Dr. Kathy Koch teaches that resiliency is a learned beha~~~~ ~~~ ~~~ ~~~~~ ~~~~~~~~~ ~~~~~~ ~~ the best strategies to help raise resilient, thriving childr~~~ ~~~~~~~~ ~~~~~~~~~~~ ~~~~~ ment. Parents will benefit from powerful, biblical str~ ~~~~~~~~~~~ ~~~~~~~~~~ their children.

KATE BATTISTELLI, author of *The God Dare* and *Growin~*

If you want your children to not give up on themselve~ ~~~~~~~~ ~~~~~~~~~~ ~~~~~~ way, read *Resilient Kids*. Dr. Kathy's ideas about spi~~~~~~~ ~~~~~~~~~~ ~~~~ help children prioritize their relationship with Christ ~ ~~~ ~~~~~~ ~~~~~~~~~ ~~~~~~ ~~~ g changers. With this incredible book, we have practical ways to help our kids. They need this. So do yours.

DAVID AND JASON BENHAM, nationally acclaimed entrepreneurs, bestselling authors, speakers

When bad things happen, some people recoil. Others rise. Kathy's book, full of character-building ideas and conversation starters, helps us coach our kids to come back stronger, wiser, and more confident after life throws them curveballs.

JIM DALY, President, Focus on the Family

Wisdom in *Resilient Kids* equips parents to raise kids who bounce back quickly from problems and think more positively about themselves. Dr. Kathy provides parents the tools and confidence to tackle the problems facing children today.

RYAN DOBSON, REBEL Parenting

From toxic positivity, zapping, self-talk, and big T and little t trauma, Dr. Kathy handles difficult parenting issues head-on in another one of her relatable books. If you are looking for solid guidance on how to raise your children to be resilient, this book is a great resource in your parental toolbox.

CANDICE DUGGER, founder of Bullied, Broken Redeemed

Dr. Kathy Koch truly knows children from the inside out and is magnificent at equipping parents, teachers, and coaches! This is a "must have" resource for adults wanting to inspire confidence and build resilience in children! The structure, examples, recommendations, and practical tools she provides make this an easy-to-follow and worth-every-minute resource you'll want to read from cover to cover!

DANNY HUERTA, VP of Parenting and Youth at Focus on the Family

This carefully crafted book can save a young person's future and life! There are so many truths that can transform thinking and behaviors. Dr. Koch gives strong, godly direction you will benefit from.

GREGORY L. JANTZ, founder of The Center • A Place of HOPE; author of 40 books

Only five generations removed from the "greatest generation," our children and grandchildren could rightly be described as the weakest. Indeed, they are more prone to mental illness, unable to adapt to adversity, no longer faith-centric, defined by despair, and relativistic at their core. Parents and grandparents are worried! Thankfully, Dr. Kathy Koch's stunning composition, *Resilient Kids*, provides the antidote! Her research paves the way forward and helps us comprehend our moment, develop essential skills to raise resilient kids, and pass along the tools of faith resiliency so desperately needed.

JEREMIAH J. JOHNSTON, Associate Pastor of Apologetics and Cultural Engagement, Prestonwood Baptist Church; president, Christian Thinkers Society

Preparing children for a world like ours, which seems to change faster and more frequently than ever, is a key to excellent parenting. Dr. Kathy has once again given parents an insightful, practical, essential, and desperately needed resource.

JOHN STONESTREET, President of the Colson Center and author of *A Practical Guide to Culture*

One of the greatest gifts you can give your child is the ability to withstand hardships and stand firm in the face of adversity or failure. Dr. Kathy's book is an extremely well-written, timely resource that guides and equips parents and children to become confident and resilient in five significant areas: physical, intellectual, social, emotional, and spiritual. Given the current world situation, this book is a must-have for every parent "for such a time as this."

LEE ANN MANCINI, adjunct professor, South Florida Bible College and Theological Seminary; author and executive producer, Sea Kids series; podcast host of *Raising Christian Kids*

Parents often struggle with the idea of allowing our children to fail. We struggle to find a balance between protecting them and allowing them to spread their wings and fly—even if they don't stick the landing. In *Resilient Kids*, Dr. Kathy uses practical applications, relatable illustrations, and powerful strategies to help us better understand the importance of fostering resiliency in children and how to do it.

DAVID AND LESLIE NUNNERY, founders of Teach Them Diligently

When life throws us a curve, the art of bouncing back and recovering quickly is important for all of us, especially our children. When they understand that problems are opportunities to learn and mature, they'll develop flexibility and resilience. This book has the direction you need! (Don't be surprised if you learn something for yourself too!)

JILL SAVAGE, host of the *No More Perfect Podcast*; author of *No More Perfect Kids*, *No More Perfect Moms*, and *No More Perfect Marriages*

If you want your children to be brave so they'll do what's right even when it's hard, they'll need to be resilient. This allows them to bounce back when they aren't successful the first time they try something and when they're knocked down, overwhelmed, and experience heartache. Dr. Kathy's ideas will empower you to stop bubble-wrapping your children. Now they can learn from challenges and mature in their character and faith. This is most important to me and why I appreciate *Resilient Kids*. Dr. Kathy's insights about spiritual resiliency are fresh and important and worth the price of the book!

HEIDI ST. JOHN, author of *Becoming MomStrong*; host of the Heidi St. John podcast; founder of MomStrongInternational.com

Did you know there are five areas where your children need to build a mindset of resilience? Or that even in our scary, uncertain world, the risks your children take today can impact their entire lives? *Get ready to go countercultural with this outstanding book.* Kathy Koch knows kids' hearts. What's more, she knows that fear doesn't have to rule and ruin their hearts and minds. Get ready to be coached on how to help your children make choices that can fill their lives with the courage and earned wisdom they need for a special, God-honoring, resilient future.

JOHN TRENT, coauthor of *The Blessing* and *The Relationally Intelligent Child*; president, The Center for Strong Families

Resilient Kids, a powerful and practical resource, shows you how to raise a confident and resilient child who believes failure is not fatal or final, but is an opportunity to learn. Dr. Kathy, in her warm conversational style, offers parents easily applicable tools to encourage and equip you to prepare your child to navigate the world today.

LORI WILDENBERG, author or coauthor of six parenting books, including *Messy Hope: Help Your Child Overcome Anxiety, Depression, or Suicidal Ideation*

Dr. Kathy Koch's book serves as a compass to weary parents, bringing us back to what matters and helping us guide our children in becoming what God has designed them to be. You owe it to your children to read this powerful book.

TODD WILSON, www.familymanweb.com, www.thesmilinghomeschooler.com

RESILIENT
KIDS

Raising Them to Embrace Life
with Confidence

KATHY KOCH, PhD

MOODY PUBLISHERS
CHICAGO

Unless otherwise indicated, Scripture quotations are from the *ESV® Bible (The Holy Bible, English Standard Version®)*, Copyright © 2001 by Crossway, a publishing ministry of Good News Publishers. Used by permission. All rights reserved.

Scripture quotations marked (NIV) are taken from the Holy Bible, New International Version®, NIV®. Copyright © 1973, 1978, 1984, 2011 by Biblica, Inc.™ Used by permission of Zondervan. All rights reserved worldwide. www.zondervan.com The "NIV" and "New International Version" are trademarks registered in the United States Patent and Trademark Office by Biblica, Inc.™

Edited by Elizabeth Cody Newenhuyse
Interior design: Puckett Smartt
Cover design: Erik M. Peterson
Cover illustration of kid on trampoline copyright © 2022 by WHISKHEELS / Shutterstock (1987115282). All rights reserved.
Cover illustration of grass copyright © 2022 by CRStocker / Shutterstock (1898201746). All rights reserved.

All websites and phone numbers listed herein are accurate at the time of publication but may change in the future or cease to exist. The listing of website references and resources does not imply publisher endorsement of the site's entire contents. Groups and organizations are listed for informational purposes, and listing does not imply publisher endorsement of their activities.

Library of Congress Cataloging-in-Publication Data
Names: Koch, Kathy, author.
Title: Resilient kids : raising them to embrace life with confidence /
    Kathy Koch, PhD.
Description: Chicago : Moody Publishers, [2022] | Includes bibliographical
    references. | Summary: "Children need to be resilient. Furthermore, they
    need parents who help them to learn from negative experiences and who
    allow them a certain measure of struggle. In Raising Resilient Kids,
    moms and dads will learn the power and purpose of resilience and how to
    parent so as to make it more likely their children will utilize this
    character quality"-- Provided by publisher.
Identifiers: LCCN 2022011547 (print) | LCCN 2022011548 (ebook) | ISBN
    9780802429094 (paperback) | ISBN 9780802473929 (ebook)
Subjects: LCSH: Parenting--Religious aspects--Christianity. | Child
    rearing--Religious aspects--Christianity. | Resilience (Personality
    trait) in children--Religious aspects--Christianity. | BISAC: RELIGION /
    Christian Living / Parenting
Classification: LCC BV4529 .K63 2022 (print) | LCC BV4529 (ebook) | DDC
    248.8/45--dc23/eng/20220325
LC record available at https://lccn.loc.gov/2022011547
LC ebook record available at https://lccn.loc.gov/2022011548

Originally delivered by fleets of horse-drawn wagons, the affordable paperbacks from D. L. Moody's publishing house resourced the church and served everyday people. Now, after more than 125 years of publishing and ministry, Moody Publishers' mission remains the same—even if our delivery systems have changed a bit. For more information on other books (and resources) created from a biblical perspective, go to www.moodypublishers.com or write to:

Moody Publishers
820 N. La Salle Boulevard
Chicago, IL 60610

1 3 5 7 9 10 8 6 4 2

Printed in the United States of America

I dedicate this book to homeschool parents, teachers, and coaches who teach, train, and reteach children who need second, third, and fourth chances to master skills and truth. Because you don't give up on them, they won't give up on themselves. They'll learn to trust themselves as they see you trust them.

Thank you for your investment!

CONTENTS

Foreword   9

1. What Is Resiliency and Why Does It Matter?   13

2. What Do Resilient Children Believe and Why Does It Matter?   29

3. What Do Children Think About What Happened and Why
    Does It Matter?   41

4. How Struggling Helps Us   57

5. Yes, But . . .   73

6. What to Do: Conversations That Build Resiliency   87

7. What to Say: Conversations That Build Resiliency   101

8. Get Unstuck: Moving from Setback to Comeback   123

9. Spiritual Resiliency   145

    One Last Thought   171

    Appendix: Beliefs Resilient Children Have About Themselves
    and Their Parents   173

    Acknowledgments   177

    Notes   181

    About Kathy Koch, PhD, and Celebrate Kids, Inc.   187

FOREWORD

As a college athlete, a friend of mine was practicing a specific maneuver for her sport. She tried repeatedly without success. Finally, her coach advised, "Just do *something* different. *Anything*." This wise coach knew that my friend needed to risk new kinds of failure to get the breakthrough she needed and eventually got.

Risking failure and learning to improve is called *resiliency*. It is an essential trait for a successful life. Resiliency is the opposite of *fragility*, which prizes safety over risk.

Staying safe by avoiding failure seems like a good strategy in uncertain times. But if we don't take risks, we can't improve. If we don't improve, we can't grow. Without growth there is no pathway out of aimlessness and anxiety.

As the president of Summit Ministries, an organization that

trains young leaders, I am deeply concerned about the fragility I see in the rising generation. So, you can imagine how excited I was to see my friend Dr. Kathy Koch boldly address the topic in *Resilient Kids*. I cannot imagine a timelier book.

Dr. Kathy is well loved by students in our Summit Ministries' student conferences. She shares difficult truths in a caring way that helps them grow. They love her for it.

In *Resilient Kids*, Dr. Kathy offers specific, practical advice to raise children who are physically, intellectually, spiritually, emotionally, and socially resilient. She shows why certain approaches work better than others, and even provides conversation starters to overcome awkwardness and build relationship.

As Dr. Kathy points out, we were designed to be resilient. Children learn to walk by falling and getting back up. This isn't failure. It's progress.

Much of Dr. Koch's advice proceeds from the Bible, which warms my heart. The Bible's heroes experience anxiety, despair, injustice, and disappointment. They fail spectacularly. Yet the Bible is a book of growth. It shows how we can blossom into the fullness of what we were designed to be. The apostle Paul tells us to "rejoice in our sufferings, knowing that suffering produces endurance, and endurance produces character, and character produces hope" (Rom. 5:3–4).

Of course, we want kids to feel safe. But there are two kinds of safety: safety *from* growing and safety *to* grow. This second kind of safety is a worthy aim for a good life. John A. Shedd said, "A ship in harbor is safe, but that is not what ships are built for."[1]

Dr. Kathy is a wise guide for helping children thrive in times like these. As you read *Resilient Kids*, I encourage you to underline, take notes, and practice the recommended strategies. You and I were made for this moment. May this book lead to a turning away from fear and indifference to confidence and caring—for you and the kids you love.

JEFF MYERS, PHD
President, Summit Ministries

What Is RESILIENCY and Why Does It MATTER?

Mommmmmyyyyyy!!"

My scream alerted every mom in the area that a little girl was in trouble. Because I was swimming when I screamed, and sound carries over water, several moms may have found their heart in their throat.

"Mommmyyyy!!"

My mom was visiting with her sister near our lake cabin while my cousins and I swam after dinner. When they heard the second scream, they both looked to the water. My mom admitted later that she thought my cousins and I were just playing and wanted them to see something.

We weren't playing anymore.

I had been swimming underwater and felt something hit my

forehead. When breaking the water, I put my hand to my forehead. I didn't think I felt anything, but when looking at my hand, I screamed again. Blood covered it.

My mom and aunt saw the blood, too, and now came running. Blood covered my whole face. (It looked worse than it was.)

My cousins helped me to the pier and my mom saw the gash in my forehead, figuring out that a rock must have hit me. Before my screams caused them to run away, children at the property next to ours were skipping stones. We all did this, too, but not when others were swimming nearby.

My dad and brother were fishing in the middle of the lake. My mom was able to get their attention and they came back to shore. Since the bleeding wouldn't stop, my mom, dad, and I headed to a nearby hospital where I got my first stitches.

I can remember the fear that gripped my heart. I was seven or eight years old and didn't like the pain or the blood. I can also remember how well my mom and dad took care of me. I remember all the fun, incident-free days of swimming, fishing, skipping rocks, horseback riding, and campfires with s'mores.

I kept swimming that vacation. For a while after that, I checked to see if anyone was skipping rocks nearby, but my mom and dad didn't assume I would be hit by one. My mom didn't hold me close and insist I swim only if she was right there to protect me. My dad took the boat out after dinner to catch fish we'd eat the next day;

he didn't assume he needed to stay close because something terrible would happen. Just because I was hit with a rock once didn't mean it would happen again.

This is how resilient people live. They don't deny what happened, but they're also not controlled by it. They process their pain, fear, and regret so they can learn from it all. Then they move on, better because of the experience. Something negative can lead to something positive.

WHAT IS RESILIENCY?

Resiliency is swimming again after a scary and disappointing accident. It's reading out loud in front of classmates even though some laughed at mistakes you made the day before. Resiliency is dating again after being badly dumped by someone you've dated for a while. It's trying out for a sports team after not being chosen the last time.

Resiliency is going to your doctor's appointment and expecting good news because of recent test results, even though you've had devastating news in the past. It's trusting your dad not to yell if you spill your milk again, because he apologized for his reaction the last time you spilled it. Resiliency is loving your grandma well, even though

This is how resilient people live. They don't deny what happened, but they're not controlled by it.

15

your other grandma just died and you know it will hurt when you lose another grandparent.

Mindset and Process

Resilience is a mindset[1] and a process of adapting well when facing significant sources of stress.[2] It's a way of thinking, feeling, and living. For instance, resilient people understand that problems and challenges are opportunities to learn and mature and they know growth takes time.

Recovering

Resiliency is recovering readily from disappointment, failure, defeat, adversity, and trauma. Because it's a process, this recovery isn't always instant, like when you punch a childhood blow-up toy and it immediately springs back as if nothing happened. Resilient children typically don't have to work as hard as other children to recover. They bounce back. When situations are more complex and challenging, "come back" may describe the process better than "bounce back."[3]

Choice, Ability, and Character

Resiliency begins as a choice, becomes a learned ability, and then can become a part of who children are—their character.[4] Children experience disappointments, stress, and a variety of challenges.

They can choose to stand up and step out of the muck and mire. They can learn to successfully navigate the mess. With enough positive experiences, they become resilient. That's the ultimate goal—that children don't have to think about whether to be resilient. They just are.

RESILIENCY AND THE FIVE IDENTITIES

From a big picture perspective, resiliency leads to growth, progress, and success. Depending on children's interests, strengths, weaknesses, and your priorities, resiliency can develop for all five of their identities—physical, intellectual, social, emotional, and spiritual.[5] Resiliency is not an all-or-nothing proposition. Children will have stronger and weaker moments with this quality of themselves just like they do with others.

For example, if *physical* activities are enjoyable for you, you probably want your children to be resilient in that realm. If they don't make the team, you want them to try again. Your daughter might bounce right back up; your son might not. Perhaps he's perfectionistic or fearful. This doesn't mean he can't develop his skills, and it doesn't mean he'll be perfectionistic or fearful in all things. How do you respond to their losses?

Intellectual resiliency means children won't hesitate to sign up for the debate team, do extra projects even when teachers explain it will stretch them, and ask you for help with a writing assignment. Remember, your reactions to their challenges and defeats will either expand or diminish their internal resources and external support. You matter and you can do this! How do you respond to their mistakes?

Social resiliency is necessary because you don't want your children to isolate or avoid activities with friends and family. It causes children to handle teasing, gossip, and criticism better than others do. They won't stay down long or assume that all people will treat them badly just because a few do. How do you respond to their conflicts?

Children who manage their feelings well have *emotional* resiliency. They won't be afraid to laugh and cry with people. Depression, stress, and anxiety won't overwhelm them typically or last as long. They won't allow themselves to be defined by negative experiences or interactions. Resiliency is strong protection against mental health struggles.[6] How do you respond to their tears?

If you want your children to have a vibrant and growing relationship with God and the church, *spiritual* resiliency may be the most important resiliency to prioritize. When children are resilient in this domain, they appropriately credit God for the good times and understand He allows the "bad times." These children may be less likely to give up when things are hard, but instead learn to persevere in prayer.[7] How do you respond to their doubts?

In addition to resiliency's value in these important identity categories, these specific benefits will encourage you to prioritize raising resilient children:

- It leads to growth and prevents perfectionism.
- It leads to hope and prevents victim mentality.
- It leads to learning and prevents plateauing and mediocrity.
- It leads to creative problem solving and prevents children from giving up.
- It leads to healthy character, including teachability, and prevents disobedience.
- It leads to confidence and prevents fear and whiny, complaining behavior.
- It leads to healthy relationships and prevents anger, blaming others, and pride.
- It causes openness and connection and prevents long-lasting depression and anxiety.
- It leads to healthy dependence and independence and prevents apathy and isolation.

WHAT MAKES RESILIENCY POSSIBLE?

You make resiliency possible. Does that excite or intimidate you? Maybe it's a bit of both. That's understandable. Parents are absolutely the key. Why?

Resiliency requires that children rely on both internal resources and external support.[8] They need to discover and develop their emotional stamina, hope, and positive character. But they won't tap into their inner resources and develop more of them if you don't expect them to and give them chances to use them. They need opportunities to use what they have and to be who they are.

You're the Essential Support

Inner strength isn't enough. No matter how strong any of us are, we need to know we will be supported by people close to us who are on our side. This is especially true for children. If your children made a list of trustworthy people, I pray you'd be at the top. Maybe you wouldn't have been a while back and that motivated you to read this book. I'm proud of you for being teachable! It's never too late to learn new beliefs and behaviors. You can learn when to run to them when they yell, "Mommy!!" and when to wait and discern if they really need you.

No matter how strong any of us are, we need to know we will be supported by people close to us who are on our side.

Your children do need to know you're there for them. You can earn their trust. Tell them the truth, teach them rather than telling and yelling, willingly enter into their pain, and share about Jesus and His ways. You're their primary support! This is a reason God gave you these children to raise.

For your children to discover and learn that they can rely on their internal strength and external support, you need to give them space to struggle. You can't bubble wrap them or hover like a helicopter over them. You need to trust them to come out stronger on the other side of their trauma. And you need to trust God and yourself.

You're the scaffolding that holds up your children while they work to repair their weaknesses. You're the solid foundation under their stumbling feet, their training wheels that get them moving in the right direction, and the networker who introduces them to other people who can support them well. You're their strategist who teaches them how to humble themselves and rely on smart strategies and systems that work.

Developing internal resources and external support allows children to weather difficulties and take intentional action so they can get through difficult moments.[9] Action is the goal. Talk about it. Expect it. Watch for it. Celebrate it!

Love Them Unconditionally

Loving your children unconditionally is one of the best ways to be there for them. You might have thought of that when reading the above section. It's a popular response when I ask parents what they think helps children become resilient. But what is it exactly?

This powerfully important love is love without limitations. It's absolute and unchanging. When you love children unconditionally, there's nothing they can do that would cause you to love them less, *and* there's nothing they can do that would cause you to love them more. You may be sad, heartbroken, and disappointed by their attitudes, choices, and behavior—many times, you may be proud of them and thrilled with their growing maturity—but, because you love without conditions, none of this changes your love for them.

In 1 Corinthians 13 we read a practical and inspiring passage about love. It's shared during many weddings. What would happen if you applied the truths to your children? For example, verse 7 reads, "Love bears all things, believes all things, hopes all things, endures all things." And just in case that's not clear, the beginning of verse 8 nails it: "Love never ends." *This* is unconditional love.

This love frees children to risk learning because they know if they don't understand something right away, your love for them will not change. They can lose a game, make a mistake during a recital, come to you seeking advice about a difficult relationship, and be honest about their cheating because they are secure in your love. When you're positioned to help them, guide them, lead them, and teach them, they'll listen! They'll be safer and more comfortable sharing their heartache, confusion, anger, and victories with you.

Unconditional love is like a good trampoline—there are side supports that prevent children from falling off and hurting themselves. Love requires boundaries. When you say no to your children and allow consequences to do their work because of mistakes and disobedience, you are loving your children. And trampolines also have good elasticity that makes bouncing safe, fun, and even necessary. Simply walking across a trampoline will put a bounce in your steps. Unconditional love does this, too.

Of course, God loves us unconditionally. This is how we know it's a precious love. We've experienced it in the most profound way. He loved us from the beginning—before we could "perform" for Him. We never need to. I praise Him for the freedom, peace, and joy that is birthed and maintained in this love! And this includes clear boundaries of what's best for us. Knowing the path to walk on is part of love.

If we ever doubt God's love, reading Psalm 136 (especially out loud) can change us and boost our confidence. The phrase "His steadfast love endures forever" is repeated twenty-six times. Another go-to passage for me is Micah 7:18—"Who is a God like you, pardoning iniquity and passing over transgression for the remnant of his inheritance? He does not retain his anger forever, because he delights in steadfast love." When you unpack the meaning of "steadfast" you see that it means loving devotion, goodness, kindness, and faithfulness.

ZIPPING THE ZIPPER! HOW KIDS PROBLEM SOLVE

On cold, snowy days, the second graders I taught arrived bundled in snowsuits with the necessary add-ons of boots, hats, and mittens. Some also had scarves. When it was time for recess or to go home at the end of the day, it took all my self-control to stand back and watch them put everything on. Or, *try* to put everything on.

I encouraged children to help each other when help was needed. I was there to support them, but I did it quietly. I might have been able to dress all twenty-eight kids faster than watching them bundle themselves back up, but I knew the struggle would pay off.

They figured out that putting their snowpants on first was smart. They learned putting their boots on was easiest if they didn't zip their coats shut first. And they learned to zip their zippers before putting on their mittens.

I loved watching them problem solve and figure things out. I was encouraged when they eventually remembered the best sequence and were able to get dressed more quickly each time.

They became resilient problem solvers. They learned to ask for specific help from friends and receive it without it making them feel stupid. They became more confident and less whiny.

I chose to lower my standard and I became confident in my students. It couldn't be about their perfection. They never would have tried to bundle themselves up if it was about pleasing me. It had to be about them being warm enough to go outside.

We must prioritize resilience because we know it benefits children today and in the future. The goal has to be for them to learn how to do things for themselves, not that the task get done perfectly.[10] They may struggle more but it will be good for them.

WHAT'S YOUR "SNOWSUIT"?

Maybe for you, it's how well your children clean their bedroom. Maybe it's remembering to get everything ready for their math lesson. Perhaps you want them to remember to practice their piano pieces without being reminded a dozen times. Would you love your children to play well together and not cry and whine when they don't win a game? You can learn to set fair expectations they can achieve.

Because of how you react to your children's losses and pain, they can decide failure isn't fatal and it isn't final. Or they can decide they're terrible people, stupid, and not worthy or capable of doing better. Your healthy responses allow children to try new things again and not panic when they make mistakes.[11] Growth happens. Now it's more likely that resiliency will become a part of their character and not just something they are able to do sometimes.

If your children's first difficulties happen when they're on their own, they won't be resilient. They're likely to stay down in the valleys and not bounce back. It could be worse—they could crash and burn.

Your children can learn to be overcomers. They can be their own hero. Their experiences and victories will build their internal strength and confidence in the external support they relied on. They can do this!

EMBRACE LIFE WITH CONFIDENCE

Do you better understand the book's title now than when you began reading? Resilient children are more equipped to embrace life with confidence.

Negative experiences don't define them. They know the difference between mistakes and failure. For resilient children, mistakes are a part of life. They're a part of learning, loving, and all aspects of being and doing. Failure is not final or fatal; it is taking advantage of opportunities to learn.

What's the big deal? Life is big and glorious! It's full of potential. When children are resilient, they walk forward eager for opportunities that will strengthen them. They're not afraid of what's hard. They'll grow.

A friend, Alan, and I were texting about a mutual friend. He wrote, "He's a lot of person." When I read it, I laughed out loud. Alan was right and I think it's how resilient people view life—there's a lot to it!

Resilient children want to live—really live. They'll get as much out of experiences as they can. They may live life with abandon. This doesn't mean they'll foolishly take lots of risks. They know themselves well and are usually able to calculate risk well. They simply want to be fully present to the life they can live.

In contrast, children who lack resilience don't get as much from life. They may doubt life has much in store for them. They'll give up, give in, and stay down in the valley rather than walk out. If they're young, they will throw more temper tantrums. If they're older, depression, stress, anxiety, and suicidal thoughts can consume them.

Without confidence, growth is almost impossible. Learning, joy, and independence will be rare. Fear and doubt may rule.

Confidence and resiliency go hand in hand. When you empower children to believe in their abilities, teach them to cope with challenges, and guide them to make wise choices, they'll be confident![12]

Diamonds form under pressure.

And let us not grow weary of doing good,
for in due season we will reap, if we do not give up.
Galatians 6:9

What Do Resilient Children **BELIEVE** and Why Does It **MATTER?**

W ow!" "Really?" "That's cool!!"
These were common responses of the second graders
I taught when they learned how powerful and fast train engines
were. I loved teaching, and especially had a good time with our
transportation unit. Our school was near railroad tracks, so teaching them about trains was enjoyable. My students were familiar
with trains and curious about them, but lacked information.

We learned about train engines and the caboose and freight
cars in between. I wrote "we" because until I taught the unit, I
didn't know what the different train cars were called and what they
likely carried. I can still remember my students' enthusiasm when
I announced that we'd go to nearby tracks one day to have a picnic
and watch the trains.

As the engine is the force powering the train, beliefs are the force causing us to do what we do. Beliefs are our internal engine. If we want children to be resilient, they'll need to believe certain things about God, themselves, others, success, failure, effort, and more. If a train can't move, check the engine. If children aren't resilient, check their beliefs.

Bouncing back quickly, asking for help, and not letting failure define them happens because of what children believe. So do panicking, hiding, blaming, and whining.

To change children's unhealthy behaviors like these, their beliefs must change. It may seem easier in the moment to focus on observable behavior, but even if their actions change, changes most likely won't last. For resiliency to become a part of who children are, you must influence their beliefs.

Why do some children panic when they get caught making a mistake and others don't? Why do some blame others while some own their part of the problem? Why do some children whine about almost everything while others don't? Ask, What do they believe?

Of course, it's fair to say that having the right beliefs is no guarantee that correct behavior will immediately follow. Children are complex and influenced by many people and things. Nerves can get in the way, someone they admire can temporarily control them, they may be unprepared for the challenge, and more. Yet we should think more about beliefs than behaviors when we want children to change. Start there.

WHAT'S A "MISTAKE"? WHAT'S A "FAILURE"?

Accurate beliefs about mistakes and failure are imperative. Parents and their children must agree on definitions so reactions to difficulties and trauma are consistent. Of all beliefs, these especially influence your children's resiliency mindset, the learning and recovery process they use, and the choices they make.

Make it a goal to parent so children understand and believe these statements:

- Mistakes happen when children do something incorrectly.[1] We can learn a lot from our mistakes. Making mistakes is not the same thing as failing.

- Failure is falling short of an expectation.[2] It's a lack of success.[3] Failure is not learning from mistakes.[4]

- Success is having the desired outcome; it's meeting the expectation.[5]

- Mistakes and failures can happen because children lack knowledge, specific abilities, and/or skills due to a lack of experience or training.

- Mistakes and failures can happen because children's attitudes get in the way or they don't use character qualities such as humility, teachability, patience, and effort.

- Many other issues can cause mistakes and failures. For example, perhaps your instruction is confusing, your expectations aren't realistic, they're not feeling well, and competition is stressful.

• Children can't be whoever or whatever they want to be. They can only be who God created them to be. Children won't be able to do everything they want to do. This doesn't mean they failed. Setting appropriate and realistic expectations is essential.[6]

KIDS AND MISTAKES

As Jill Savage and I wrote in *No More Perfect Kids*, when young children fall because they're attempting to walk, we don't tell them they made a mistake.[7] We don't think of it that way. Instead, we celebrate their efforts and encourage them to keep trying. We know progress and ultimately error-free walking will result from our encouragement and their action.

For children to grow and make progress they have to be challenged. This means they'll make mistakes. Healthy high achievers understand this, so they don't panic when they don't know something. They know they can analyze what happened and learn to do better.[8] Because we and our children can learn from mistakes, maybe we should think about "bouncing forward" instead of "bouncing back." Children may not immediately move beyond where they were, but we want them to eventually.

Of course, if we draw lots of attention to children's mistakes and make them feel bad for making them, they'll see their mistakes as more damaging than they could and should be. Mistakes simply happen as children progress toward good, better, and best.

But you may be thinking, *Don't we draw attention to children's mistakes when they stumble and fall when learning to walk?* No, not at all. I would argue that we draw attention to their *progress*. We make them feel good for trying and for improving.

Learning will involve some bumps in the road. They may fall off a trampoline. There may be challenges and hardships. Tears may fall. All of this is part of life—none of it is because the child is bad or stupid. And it's not because the parent or teacher did a bad job. Sure, adults can have an off day, and so can kids, but for the most part, mistakes are what happen before children know everything they need to know. If they don't give up, and we don't give up on them, they'll learn and perhaps master the task. We offer freedom to risk and learn when we believe this and communicate it consistently in our reactions to their mistakes. We build the resilience muscle.

FAILURE AND FEELINGS

Feeling like a failure or actually failing are main things children must learn to bounce back from. It doesn't matter if we define what they're struggling with as failure or not. And it doesn't matter if children feel they caused what went wrong or not. They feel like failures regardless.

Based on informal "research" on my Facebook page, most adults define failure as quitting. Children most often define failure as not accomplishing what they wanted or needed to do. Some included that it was because they didn't put in enough effort and many said it was because they didn't know enough.

It's good to acknowledge what you believe about failure and to ask your children for their thoughts and feelings. In the same way that Jill Savage and I wrote about perfectionism in our book, *No More Perfect Kids*, let me suggest that your thoughts and feelings about failure impact your children.

Is This About You?

Do you tend to think "Don't fail" or "Don't fail *me*"? Are you more concerned with how children's errors, disappointments, and difficulties reflect on you or hurt them? It can be both. But what's the more significant issue for you?

If it's often about your reputation and feelings, please don't feel ashamed. This is common. As I say when I'm in front of an audience, you were not responsible for any of these new ideas yesterday, but you are responsible for them in the future. My goals are to help you understand why your feelings have been getting in the way and to give you hope that change is possible.

Children will make mistakes and may fail and find themselves in hard places because they have a lot to learn. You could be the best parent ever, and your children would still struggle. And they should. They'll be stronger for it. I'm guessing you know that, but you still want to prevent them from experiencing pain.

Is Protecting Them Wise?

Of course! Your heart is that they wouldn't be hurt by anyone or anything. But, let me suggest that by protecting them now, you're making it more likely that they'll experience real aches and pains later. That's because we develop everything from hard skin to healthy comebacks to discernment to confidence when we rebound from disappointments and heartache. Overprotecting kids means they won't learn how to come back while they're in the safety of your home—rather, they'll have to figure it out when they're on their own. But they may not ever figure it out. They may just stay down in the valley because they haven't learned how to rise from it.

Jessica Lahey came face to face with the dangers of not letting her children experience failure when her oldest child entered middle school. As an experienced middle school teacher, she had seen behavior patterns in students that concerned her. Now she saw them in her child and made important connections. She investigated and wrote a compelling and challenging book that includes these conclusions:

> We have taught our kids to fear failure, and in doing so, we have blocked the surest and clearest path to their success.[9]

35

Today's overprotective, failure-avoidant parenting style has undermined the competence, independence, and academic potential of an entire generation.[10]

I have inadvertently extended my children's dependence in order to appropriate their successes as evidence and validation of my parenting.[11]

Could I suggest that you slowly reread those three statements? How do you react? Based on what you've observed in other children, your children, and what you've read so far, do you strongly agree or not agree much at all? How relevant are they for you? After you read each sentence, create a next sentence that starts with "Therefore . . ." How you complete that sentence will tell you a lot about your current perspective.

"BIG T" TRAUMA AND "LITTLE T" TRAUMA

Mental health professionals talk about "big T" trauma and "little t" trauma.[12] It's appropriate to acknowledge that some negative experiences are more brutal than others. Coming back isn't always easy.

"Little t" Trauma

Some define "little t" trauma as things that threaten children's egos.[13] This would include not earning an A on a test after telling everyone you would. Being teased for an outfit you wore to a youth group activity would also be considered "little t trauma." Forgetting part of a memorized piano song during a recital and being selected last for a team during a PE class also qualify. When "little t" experiences repeat regularly, children's pain and reactions can be similar to "big T" trauma.

"Big T" Trauma

Life-threatening trauma is defined as "big T" trauma. This would include suicide attempts, entering rehab for an addiction, the death of a parent, dropping out of school because of bullying, and any kind of abuse.

I hope you agree that strong faith and a vibrant relationship with God can change "big T" trauma to "little t" trauma in the minds and hearts of His followers. For example, friends of mine have sailed through cancer treatment. Not everyone has that experience. Relying on the strength and comfort only God provides also makes enduring and coming through the terrible loss of a parent or spouse more manageable. Don't get me wrong, the losses are real and the cancer treatment was tough, but their choice to believe God and rely on Him made all the difference.

Major or Minor

Categorizing children's struggles isn't essential but it helps you realize the inner resources and external support they'll need. You also need to remember your children are individuals. They won't respond the same way to the same negative experiences. Something minor to one might be major to another. Neither reaction is necessarily wrong. An individual's past experiences, the value they place on success in a given area, their opinions about the event and the people involved, and how they perceive their responsibility in the situation are all relevant.

Moving beyond Experiences

No matter what's happened, our goal must be to help children move beyond the experience. There may be a two-steps-forward-one-step-back reality, and that's fine. One child might be affected longer than another by the death of a grandparent, not making a sports team, falling and embarrassing himself in front of peers, or by an older sibling moving out.

Most children will have more "little t" experiences than "big T" ones. Suppose they learn to handle the minor trauma well and learn from their experiences, strengthen and expand their inner resources, turn to support around them for help, and more. In that case, they'll better manage "big T" experiences when they encounter them. This is why I'm emphasizing "little t" experiences more in this book. Of course, increasing confidence to navigate both is essential for children to embrace life.

EMBRACE LIFE WITH CONFIDENCE

Beliefs are your engine, and they're your children's engine. They move you. They give you and them power and energy to act. I trust you see the relevance of beliefs about mistakes and failure. If they're not healthy, embracing life is unlikely.

What about what your children believe about themselves and about you? These beliefs are significant too! You'll benefit from making a list of what you realize they should believe. You can base it on your life experiences, what motivated you to read this book, and what you've read so far.

I've started a list of beliefs for you in the appendix. You could look at it now, add to it, or start making a list before you read mine. What your children believe about themselves and you can cause their resilience or deny them this gift. Their beliefs can cause them to embrace life or run from it.

———————

**Bumblebees appear to defy the physics of aerodynamics.
They don't know they shouldn't be able to fly, so they fly.**

The steadfast love of the LORD never ceases;
his mercies never come to an end; they are new every
morning; great is your faithfulness.
Lamentations 3:22–23

What Do Children Think About What HAPPENED and Why Does It MATTER?

When you're disappointed because something happened to your daughter, have you caught her spinning quite a tall tale to explain it? "She made me do it!" "The teacher never told us about the test!" "I'm the only one not chosen and I'll never forgive my teacher!"

Perhaps you caught your son making up excuses when telling you about something good that happened. It's as if he doesn't want to own his strengths. Maybe he can't. "I was so lucky and I'll never be able to do it again!" "I got a part in the play, but I'm not any good. I'm going to be terrible! It's just that no one good tried out." "I'm not as depressed as I used to be, but I'm sure it's only because that mean kid moved."

Children, like adults, tell themselves stories to try to make sense of problems and successes. Their stories reveal their "explanatory style."[1] Resilient children have an optimistic explanatory style that decreases their stress. Non-resilient children are much more pessimistic and can be prone to depression.

EXPLANATORY STYLE MATTERS

Paying attention to children's style is important because what they believe influences how they approach and respond to challenges, failures, and trauma. If you discover that the story they tell themselves is unhealthy and untrue, you can intervene. Help them believe accurate perspectives about their past, present, and future challenges. They can then become more optimistic and more resilient. Without overcoming the lies with truth, chances are they won't grow.

Be aware that children can be resilient and optimistic during athletics and not when learning the piano. Or it might be the other way around. And they might have a different explanatory style for their obedience than their academic pursuits. The same is true for adults. It depends on how strong and healthy that identity component is—past experiences, the people involved, and our attitudes and abilities.

Let's look at the three elements of explanatory style as developed by Martin Seligman[2] and demonstrated in this sample whining statement. I'll add a fourth element that you must understand to help your children bounce forward. Then I'll also show you how the story you tell yourself about your children's struggles matters greatly. Yes, you have an explanatory style!

It's alllll my fault! I'll never get over it! My whole life is ruined!!

Does this sound familiar? These are common beliefs and re-actions from non-resilient children. They blame themselves, they can't change, the pain will last forever, and it will affect everything.

Listen for these kinds of all-inclusive statements so you can have honest conversations about them. Telling children "You don't have to feel that way, get over it" and "Be realistic" won't help. Showing them truths about what happened, and teaching and especially demonstrating healthy responses, will help you and your child.

Personalization: Who Is Responsible?

Explanatory style includes who is to blame. Pessimistic children tend to blame themselves when bad things happen and give credit to others when good things happen. They usually believe they're incapable of change. It's the opposite for optimists who take ap-propriate credit for good events and can see their role in what went wrong. They're also quick to understand how others influenced the bad events.

There are huge differences between "There was nothing I could have done," "The bully made me hit him," and "I could have re-mained calm instead of getting angry." In children's reasons, you can learn to see where blame is placed and whether there's evidence of resiliency. You'll get insights into approaching your concerns and your child's attitudes and actions.

You want children to be honest about their part in a dilemma. Did they forget to do their homework or intentionally decide not to do it? Are children quick to blame siblings for the mess in the den that made their grandparents mad when they are just as much to blame? Does your son whine incessantly about an umpire's call rather than taking responsibility for the fact that he was called out on strikes?

Personalization	Bad Events	Good Events
Non-Resilient Pessimists	Internal sources (They blame themselves.) "I'm clueless."	External sources (They credit others.) "My teammates are quick!"
Resilient Optimists	External sources (They accurately blame others.) "I didn't have good role models."	Internal sources (They appropriately credit themselves.) "I'm quick!"

Change Is Possible

You can be fully present to your children and attentive with your ears and eyes so you get ideas about what caused the problem. Then you can speak up and correct your children's misunderstandings. Be honest about how others behaved without throwing them under the bus. Kindly point out how your children's beliefs, attitudes, and actions contributed to the problem. And teach your children what they can do differently next time that can result in a better outcome. It doesn't do them much good to know they're part of the problem. They need to know and believe they can change.[3]

Children who take responsibility for their part of negative experiences are more resilient than those who don't.[4] So when you make it safe for your children to admit what happened, their resiliency muscle is strengthened. As they discover they can learn from the experience and you won't shame them, taking responsibility for their choices and attitudes won't be as risky. Now they can become more optimistic and that changes everything. (The way you communicate is significant to whether children will feel safe. I'll address this in chapter 5.)

We don't want our children to only blame others when they're at least partly responsible, but we also don't want them always assuming they're in the wrong. For instance, if a boyfriend is always late picking up your daughter, you don't want her to believe she's worthless and that he's late because of her. She benefits from seeing his character flaw for what it is. Be ready and available to point this out carefully.

Permanence: How Long Will It Last?

How long the fallout from a traumatic or difficult event will last is another element included in the story children create. Will the effects be temporary or permanent? Resilient and optimistic children believe good events have permanent causes and bad events have temporary causes. Therefore, they expect more good things to occur and to be able to overcome bad things.

Non-resilient, pessimistic children believe good things have temporary causes and probably can't be repeated. They believe bad things have permanent causes so their problems and pain will last forever. Because they think they can't control or change the reasons, they're known for complaining, giving up, and resisting trying again. They don't think trying will help.

For example, non-resilient children will think of themselves as permanently stupid rather than just careless during a test. They'll think of themselves as bad kids rather than just disobedient one time. Do you see the permanence of these negative beliefs? No wonder they keep struggling and seem unable or unwilling to work on attitudes and actions we know would help them.

Permanence	Bad Events	Good Events
Non-Resilient Pessimists	Permanent causes "My dad never knows what he's doing!"	Temporary causes "I was lucky!"
Resilient Optimists	Temporary causes "My dad made a mistake today."	Permanent causes "I knew what to study and it paid off!"

Change Is Possible

Take care of yourself so you can be optimistic even when facing more of the same negative encounters and experiences. Find something positive even when your children are disappointed repeatedly—perhaps because they're not growing yet in their ability to take responsibility for their part of the problem and they're sure "nothing will ever change." Believe good is coming. Look forward with hope! If you can't, neither will they.

Observe your children's optimistic and pessimistic reactions to people and events. Listen for how they communicate and ask questions. What's their tone of voice? What words do they use? Some children may appear to be optimistic much of the time, but you may discover that their views toward their struggles are ruled by pessimism. You won't want to miss this. It's controlling them and they need to know that.

If your children are sure their pain will last forever, mark the day on a calendar when the disappointment began. Now, pay close attention to your children's attitudes and behaviors. Make notes about their shifts so you can tell them they've become happier, more content, less anxious, and anything else you notice. When negatively oriented children don't believe they'll ever improve or be satisfied, they can't recognize positive changes. They'll continue to have a woe-is-me attitude.

I'm not suggesting you hurry grief along in all cases. Grief is a process and we know it takes time. I just don't want your children sitting down in a valley they're meant to walk through. I want them to bounce back, come back, and bounce forward. This will require more optimism toward themselves and their situations.

Also, note when the same old causes don't influence your children in the way they would have in the past. Now make time to talk about both the shift in their attitudes and the successes they've had. Evidence doesn't lie! Take pictures, save old and new schoolwork, and get insights about your children's behavior and choices from teachers and coaches. These can convince children that they're telling themselves an old story—a wrong story. Now resiliency in the future may be possible.

Pervasiveness: How Will It Affect Them?

Do you remember the example I used at the beginning of this chapter? The child loudly declared, *My whole life is ruined!!* He or she views their difficulties and challenges as catastrophic. For children with this pervasive explanatory style, everything looks bleak. They react to what we consider "little t" trauma as "big T" trauma. They're non-resilient pessimists. They catastrophize their lives and expect the bad things that happened in English class to affect math and even after-school activities and clubs. What went wrong at 9:30 a.m. will be the excuse for anything else that goes wrong that day.

The optimistic, resilient children believe the opposite of this explanatory style. They tend to compartmentalize life's events. They believe bad things are bumps in the road and not major catastrophes. They don't expect negative encounters to bleed over into other parts of their lives, so they don't. English is English. Math is math. And drill team practice doesn't have anything to do with either one.

Pervasiveness	Bad Events	Good Events
Non-Resilient Pessimists	Universal causes "All coaches are bad."	Specific cases "I'm creative during art class."
Resilient Optimists	Specific cases "My coach had a bad day."	Universal causes "I'm creative."

Change Is Possible

Would it surprise you to know my advice is the same as I offered above? Listen and look so you can affirm children's healthy beliefs and redirect their thinking when necessary. For instance, if they whine much more than you think is appropriate for the struggle they're facing, ask them why. Why has it become a big deal to them? If it hasn't, talk about more appropriate reactions to their challenge.

Realize that resilient children who don't expect one adverse event to affect everything may appear to come back and even bounce forward easily. They often will, but be present in case they would benefit from processing feelings with you. There's still pain and disappointment they need to face. Sometimes quickly bouncing back is actually running from the pain. Learn to recognize the difference.

Help your daughter realize a friendship struggle doesn't have to affect her grades even if the peer in question shares classes with her. Help your son see that one bad basketball game doesn't mean the next one will also go badly. Help your youngest see that forgetting about a math test doesn't have to ruin his whole math semester grade and it doesn't mean he'll forget history and science tests in the future.

Look for patterns and keep a written record. Perhaps showing your non-resilient son who catastrophizes everything that his grades have gone up since the one horrible test experience will help him learn to compartmentalize bad events.

Maybe you will see a pattern of one or two of your daughter's former friends being a negative influence in various ways. This evidence will help to empower your daughter to further distance herself from them. When she sees that other friends haven't had the same effect, she'll be able to classify those former friends differently from others.

Recovery: What Will It Require?

Part of children's explanatory story includes whether bouncing back from the defeat and trauma is possible. Resilient children believe they can and must overcome negative events. Pessimistic non-resilient children will most likely think there's nothing they can do because of the permanence of the causes, the universal reasons they blame, and the personal responsibility they own for the problems.

What will it take to recover?	Bad Events
Non-Resilient Pessimists	"There's nothing I can do."
Resilient Optimists	"I'll do whatever it takes."

Change Is Possible

Everything I've written above is relevant to helping children walk out of their valleys. Everything *you do* to increase their optimism and shift their perspectives will help them believe there are things *they can do*. Then teaching "those things" will give rise to their hope and optimism. There's much in the upcoming pages to help you.

Ask Your Children

You can discover your children's explanatory style by asking these four questions. Answers will help you see their pessimistic, non-resilient behavior or their optimistic, resilient behavior. Now you'll know how to prepare yourself for their future struggles and be better able to respond to them well.

Do they most consistently take responsibility for their parts of problems or blame others?

Do they believe the causes of problems and the pain caused by them will be permanent or temporary?

Do they expect the problem to permeate many areas of their lives or affect just the area where the problem occurred?

Do they believe they can make changes to overcome the issue and prevent it from happening again?

What about You?

As you read about your children's explanatory styles, did you think about yours? You have one. You could go back and reread this entire section with yourself in mind. Do you think your children make mistakes because you're a terrible parent? Are you the cause? Are you permanently "bad"?

Have you felt responsible for the hurt a daughter experienced? Was it your fault? Is that the story you tell yourself and why you won't let her do things independently?

Do you believe you must protect your children from all difficulties? Is this why you limit their activities and panic if they tell you about negative things?

Do you believe bouncing back is too hard and not worth it? Is this why you don't encourage your children to put forth more effort?

Ouch! If this was hard to read, remember you aren't responsible for what you do not know. You don't need to feel shame or blame. Rather, be grateful for what you're learning and focus on the future.

EMBRACE LIFE WITH CONFIDENCE

Helping your children know the God of the Bible and see Him for who He is may be the best way to help them embrace life well. Optimism and hope come from God the Father, Jesus His Son, and the Holy Spirit. He can build their resiliency. He can build yours too. I hope you know Him. He has changed everything for me.

How would you want your children to depend on God? Why should they? When learning new things? When struggling to overcome heartache? When deciding who to blame for something troublesome? When wondering if a problem is a bump in the road or a catastrophe? When working to understand if challenges will always be a part of their lives? When deciding whether to give up or work on improving?

Do your children blame God when things go badly? Or do they turn to God when things go badly? What do they need to know?

Do your children ignore God when things go well? Or do they praise Him when things go well? What do they need to know?

God's presence, power, provision, and protection rock my world. If you know Him and His Word, talk with your children about these four attributes. Think of others. What does He do for us and what do we do to appropriate it all?[5]

**It looks like nothing is going on in a compost pile.
It's full of garbage, and it's full of life!**

"It's not whether you get knocked down, it's whether you get up."
— Coach Vince Lombardi[6]

How STRUGGLING Helps Us

The newborn giraffe struggled and struggled. Watching it is among my favorite international memories.

After teaching missionaries at a conference in Niger, Africa, our local hosts took some of us to a giraffe preserve. Never in our wildest imagination did we think we'd get to experience what we did.

When standing among about two hundred giraffes, we saw that one of them was about to deliver. How could we tell? We saw two of the baby's legs coming out of the birth canal just before the soon-to-be mother calmly sauntered away from the tower. (Isn't that the best name for a herd of giraffes?!)

Our assigned guide was sure he knew where it was going, so he quickly drove us in his jeep through fields and around trees. After parking, he scampered to the top of a tree to see if he had correctly predicted the giraffe's location. He also explained we couldn't get close unless the giraffe had given birth.

I still remember how excited we were when he climbed down and told us he was right, the baby had arrived, and we could get close if we were quiet. Of course, we could be quiet!

We walked carefully around trees and over downed limbs from the parked jeep to arrive at a well-hidden clearing about ten minutes after the baby was born. The statuesque mother stood on guard. She immediately noticed us and always turned her head in our direction when we whispered, quietly laughed, or she heard a camera click. She made it clear she'd protect her baby at all costs.

The baby tried to lift its heavy neck and stand and nurse. It wasn't going through that struggle for insignificant reasons—it had to stand to live. Its effort was life-giving.

God creates the giraffe to know it needs to nurse and how to do it. Amazing! The baby knows it must first lift its head and neck and then trust its newborn legs to stand.

We chuckled as the baby tried again and again. Its neck was like a piece of wet spaghetti. It would rise halfway and then quickly fall. The baby would try again almost immediately.

Occasionally the mother bent its neck down and gracefully nudged the baby, sometimes licking it. It couldn't lift the baby's neck to nurse, and it wouldn't help to lie down. The mother had to wait, simply providing quiet support. Eventually the baby was able to keep its neck upright and was strong enough to stand. The mother positioned herself and the baby knew what to do. Nursing immediately commenced.

Life would be easier if children understood the necessity of struggling the same way baby giraffes understand. They'd know what to do and eagerly try repeatedly until they were successful. They would realize giving up isn't a possibility. Initiative, effort, diligence, and perseverance would be necessary and progress would be easier.

Of course, you'd have to understand some things too. Standing by and being supportive is your role. Not doing everything for your child is healthy, and not helping with every little thing will bring about more success. Helping them for the long term is what a good parent does.

THE VALUE OF FACING CHALLENGES

As you're discovering, resiliency is possible and probable when children believe certain things. But even with healthy beliefs, if children don't see any value in challenges, they may do a U-turn at the beginning of every valley. Even if they have the experience and ability to handle a challenge, they may decide it's not worth the effort.

Not trying new things, not asking for help, giving up, and hiding their pain will become your children's norm. They'll plateau and not grow. If they go on like that, they'll barely be living.

Growth will not be likely, but apathy could be. Joy will not be likely, but depression could be. Confidence will not be likely, but fear could be. Healthy relationships will not be likely, but comparison and jealousy could be.

Of course, all that I've written is also true for you. When you embrace any changes you need to make to be your healthiest, you *and* your children benefit. If you're not resilient, it will be difficult for your children to be.

You know your children are affected by your attitudes, beliefs, and actions. They're like wet cement and everything makes an impression. They're watching you handle your "little t" and "big T" trauma. Through your role modeling, you're teaching.[1] Therefore, I encourage you to believe you *and* your children can and will benefit from challenges and difficulties.

We don't become robust and equipped to live well when everything comes easily to us or we're handed everything on a silver platter. Many of us value most the things we worked hard to accomplish. I don't want children robbed of this beauty. This means we have to allow them to learn things the hard way sometimes. It means we have to step back and allow them to figure things out sometimes just as giraffe moms let their babies learn on their own. But I am not suggesting that you create horribly difficult situations for your children or watch them get into big trouble when you could and should absolutely prevent it. Notice that I used the word "sometimes."

Struggles Can Strengthen Trust

Trust is the foundation of all things good. Think about it. When children trust you, they'll be honest and vulnerable. You'll have more opportunities to bless and teach them. They'll willingly learn from both your actions and your words. You can be their authority, and they'll question your love less and have more hope and joy. Trust secures their heart.[2]

Handling challenges well builds trust. If children have no mountains to climb and no rapids to navigate, they don't need anyone to trust. If life is always easy, they won't be strong in you or themselves.

Growth

My muscles don't grow when I sit at home in my recliner. They grow when I work out at the fitness center with my trainer. I trust Linda as I see her considering my back issues when making decisions. I know she's spotting me carefully when I lift weights. Because of my trust, I do what she tells me to do and I don't question her when she pushes me beyond what I think I can do.

Trust is necessary for growth. It allows children to try new things and risk not getting things right the first time. They can

61

try out for a team and not make it. They can admit they're overwhelmed with trying to write a paper. They can tell you they've been bullied, or worse.

Because you're available and helpful as needed, children can be successful. These successes allow them to ultimately trust themselves too. This must be what you want—that they trust in you so they can trust in themselves.

Do They Need You?

If you're not there for them to learn from, they can decide they don't need you. Teens have sadly told me this. They won't want you around if you shame them or yell at them. I've heard this far too often as well. If you do everything for them, they'll be dependent, but that's not the same as trust. Young people see this as interference, and it makes them angry.[3]

> **If you're not there for them to learn from, they can decide they don't need you.**

If you always caution your children and attempt to bubble-wrap them like you might a valuable vase as you pack for a move, they'll receive several messages.[4] *I'm not capable. Mom doesn't think I can do anything. I better not make any mistakes today!*

On the other hand, when you teach them what they need and walk with them through experiences, their trust grows and their identity can become, *Mom thinks I can do this. Mom trusts me. Dad can help me get better at this.* They'll learn to look within and outside themselves.

Fragile or Not?

Believe this: "Kids aren't as fragile as we tend to think. They are born with strengths and abilities to cope with adversity, learn from their mistakes, and mature into responsible, competent adults. Yet they cannot develop and activate their inner resources unless we allow them opportunities to do so."[5]

Read that last sentence again. If you try to protect children from challenges and pain, they become more fragile.[6] They won't take risks or readily try new things. They're bound to hesitate and complain when things are hard. They may become victims of their difficulties and struggle with anxiety and stress.

Children who successfully handle "little t" trauma because you expect them to *and* you provide support are less likely to panic when faced with "big T" trauma. Of course, it will still be hard, but they'll remember they're strong, powerful, loved, and supported. They're appropriately independent and dependent.

Your job is to walk with your children through difficulties and disappointments. When you're connected and engage with them to feel their feelings and help them solve their problems, they can discover how very capable they are.[7]

When you're the one cheering "You can do it!" *and* teaching them how *and* allowing them to learn from mistakes, they learn they can trust you. Your relationship will be so much more solid than if you overprotect them.

To build trust, stop bubble-wrapping your children or hovering over them. If you let them struggle, they won't trust you less. They'll ultimately trust you more. And this changes everything, because without trust growth is almost impossible.

Three Approaches

1. If you've been doing too much for your children, decide to step back. Or, if you've abandoned them or yelled when they get into trouble and you know these habits have also made trust hard, tell them you're going to change because it's best for them and you. If you don't tell them, your changes will confuse them. And telling them makes it more likely you will work to change.

2. If you recognize you're meeting some of your needs by ensuring your children don't falter, talk with someone who can help you. What are you afraid of? Do you think all of their struggles reflect poorly on you? How have you learned this?

3. If you're in the habit of helping too soon and too much, leave the room if you can. Set a timer on your phone to remind yourself to check on your children in a few minutes. Help them if you believe they have tried and truly need you.

Struggles Can Mature Children's Character

Struggles improve children's character, affecting all their identities—emotional, social, intellectual, physical, and spiritual.[8] Their identity becomes "I can" instead of "I can't," "I will" instead of "I won't," "I did" instead of "I didn't."

When children experience challenges, they are "forced" to discover their inner strengths, passions, goals, and abilities. They can become strong and confident. They know they're brave, and they may see themselves as invincible. They know they can solve problems. The next time they're faced with one, they won't panic or be afraid.

Growing through challenges teaches children that initiative, effort, diligence, and perseverance are necessary because not all learning is easy. Not all of life is easy either. Children learn they need these qualities because they want to embrace life and do well. They don't need these qualities because they lack ability or experiences. They're not stupid. The opposite is true. Understanding this can change everything.

What Would You Say?

In fact, when speaking about resiliency, I ask my audience to raise their hands if their character has been positively affected by challenging experiences. The vast majority of them raise their hands and it doesn't take them long to do so. Many testify to the truths of

65

Romans 5:3—suffering does produce endurance. Endurance does produce additional character qualities. Then we find hope.

You might think of times in your life when your healthy character qualities became real to you. Maybe you could have cheated like most others in your class, but you didn't. Then they teased you. You learned you are honest and you won't let yourself be bullied into things. Maybe you were aggressively harassed at the workplace, but you didn't give in or give up. You learned who you are and found ways to protect yourself. You developed self-respect, a new level of gratitude that you were safe, and compassion for yourself and others.

In the same way, when children have to struggle and navigate disappointments, their character can mature. When they're supported by you and develop inner resources because of challenges they face, they're stronger for it. Of course, hopefully nothing horrific happens to them. If it does, and they're learning to be resilient, have hope that their character gains will daily serve them well.

Three Approaches

1. If your children are in the habit of complaining that things are too hard, find new ways of reacting so they learn the value of effort.[9] Make sure you model that effort and diligence are admirable qualities and simply are a part of life when we live on purpose.

2. Ask your children if they believe needing to use qualities like

perseverance means they're stupid or smart. Explain why you see perseverance and other character qualities as signs of wisdom and maturity. Work to get as much buy-in as possible.

3. When your children successfully walk out of valley experiences and navigate a hostile encounter, point out which character qualities they used. Avoid telling them they're "good," but instead tell them if they were gentle, discerning, careful, and kind. (I elaborate on how to compliment children in chapter 6.)

Struggles Can Enhance Children's Future

When you help children be okay with "sitting in discomfort,"[10] they won't run when struggling or disappointed. They are likely to learn from their experiences. They'll bounce forward, believing there are important reasons to push through the challenge rather than back away from it. This only happens if they encounter difficulties and have positive recovery experiences. You can't overprotect them.

You're not raising children; you're raising adults. Right? You parent children, but you raise adults. Resiliency will serve them well. You know adulthood can be wrecked by trauma of all sorts. Difficulties and disappointments can be around every corner. Today's struggles have great payoff potential for later.

Go for it!

When children know challenges benefit them, they'll be braver as adults. They'll know about their inner resources and how to ask for and receive support. Rather than doubting and being fearful, they may go for a promotion, volunteer to serve their church in a new capacity, and willingly tackle a home improvement project.

Successfully walking out of valleys and navigating struggles results in a solution-focused mindset. They can keep the end in mind rather than getting bogged down in the details of the adverse event. This certainly serves children well. It also will enhance their future. Resilient people are resourceful and innovative, with a big bag of tricks up their sleeves.[11]

Consequences

Also, because resilient children walk through difficulties rather than giving up and becoming victims of their trauma, they discover and believe that positive and negative consequences have educational value. They learn how to predict how things may play out. They can now think, "If I let him bully me again, then this may happen." If you protect them to prevent all trauma, they won't learn these principles. They'll continue to doubt and not engage fully in life.

Successfully walking out of valleys and navigating struggles results in a solution-focused mindset.

Don't get me wrong—they won't necessarily thank you now for allowing negative consequences to play out! But later the chances are good that they'll truly see your wisdom in allowing them to discover how their decisions influence their outcomes. It will enable them to become appropriately dependent and independent at the same time. You need to believe the "educational benefits of consequences are a gift, not a dereliction of duty."[12]

Three Approaches

1. Together, learn about some successful adults who had very challenging childhoods. Talk about how they overcame a seemingly detrimental background.[13]
2. You can also learn about people who never attained the success predicted for them—partly because they had an easy life.
3. Especially if your children already have dreams and hopes for their future, talk about how their past and current "big T" and "little t" trauma is preparing them. It will be interesting to see how they respond.

EMBRACE LIFE WITH CONFIDENCE

What do you think? Am I nuts or possibly correct that struggles can benefit your children so much? What are you going to do with what you now believe?

Growing your children's trust and character and parenting with the future in mind will change them, equip them, and inspire them. All three of these areas will help them embrace life.

I've had many wonderful experiences teaching sixteen- to twenty-five-year-olds at Summit Ministries.[14] Students who attend sessions at their headquarters in Manitou Springs, Colorado, can choose to go whitewater rafting one day if they choose to. Many hesitate before signing up. Most have never done it and the descriptions and pictures can be intimidating. Some have told me they signed up, woke up, and went, but they were still nervous and not sure they'd like it.

On the river they will encounter rough waters and unavoidable rapids and scary turns. The day only works because the Summit staff contracts with a trustworthy organization to manage the experience. They know the rafts and all safety equipment are appropriate for such a trip. They know the guides are well trained and capable. They prepare the students as best they can.

At the end of the day, these students are ready to go again. It's not just that it was fun (and it was for most of them), but they admit to loving the challenge. They had to use and grow their character and they most definitely had to trust others and themselves. They recognize that bravely doing something new where they had to depend on others matured them. Some admit that probably nothing in their future will scare them now.

Maybe you and your children don't need to go whitewater rafting to be convinced that struggles will be beneficial, but is there another challenge you're facing that you could lean into?

A FINAL NOTE

Before closing this chapter, I'd be negligent if I didn't include here that struggles can radically transform your faith and the faith of your children. That's why the last chapter of the book is about spiritual resiliency. Yes, an entire chapter, because I suspect this resilience may be most important to many readers. With solid faith in the God of the Bible, Jesus, and the Holy Spirit, it's much more likely that all of life will be embraced.

Pearls form because of irritants in oysters.

Count it all joy, my brothers, when you meet trials of various kinds, for you know that the testing of your faith produces steadfastness. And let steadfastness have its full effect, that you may be perfect and complete, lacking in nothing.

James 1:2–4

Yes, BUT...

You may have agreed with a lot of what you just read in chapter 4. At least much of it makes sense to you. Yet has your internal self-talk machine shut down a lot of these ideas, these challenges, even this hope, with automatic "Yes, but..." comebacks? I get that. Depending on your experiences, past beliefs, habits, and reasons you're reading this book, you may be wrestling with a lot.

Simply knowing that children benefit from experiencing tough times doesn't mean it's easy to watch them struggle. Did you bristle at the idea that you should not try to protect your children from the tough things the world may throw at them? Maybe you yourself struggle with perceived failures or something else in your past. You don't want your kids to go through what you did.

To change how you approach your children's struggles, you

must ask yourself *why* you don't want them to struggle. What might be getting in your way? What do you believe?

A SCAR'S MESSAGE

My friend Dave Roever, a highly decorated Purple Heart recipient, thinks of his many scars as "evidence of empathy."[1] I love that! I've had three knee surgeries, so if you're facing knee surgery, my scars show you that I understand. We both know the pain, the struggle to recover, the frustration of new limits, and more. We can relate to each other and comfort each other. Being able to use my scars in this way always makes me wink at God. *I see what You're doing here. You're allowing me to use a tough situation for someone's good. Thank You!*

Living in denial isn't wise. We need to recognize we've been hurt. Healthy statements that can lead to recovery include *I'm hurting*, or *They hurt me*, or *That hurt*. Next, we need to want to heal. And we must be willing to reach out for help.

Have you ever tried to remove your own splinter? Most of us don't like to inflict pain. We're too cautious. It's almost always easier when someone else holds the tweezers and digs a bit. The same is true for bigger wounds. We're not designed to heal alone.

Scars mean we've been hurt, but we've chosen to live. I tell young people to allow God to do His healing work, to rely on faithful parents to help them heal, and to do their own work. If they don't, they could bleed to death. Or dirt could enter the open wound and they could die from an infection. (I never share any of this lightly. I always watch for nodding heads as they get the analogy.)

During surgery on our soldiers, doctors look for all the shrapnel before closing a wound. They want to find and remove

Healthy statements that can lead to recovery include **I'm hurting**, *or* **They hurt me**, *or* **That hurt.**

it all. Choosing to overcome and come back from trauma can be painful. It hurts. We might say it's not for wimps! Dave and other warriors I've met have told me about shrapnel working itself to the surface of their skin years after their initial injury and surgery. It always irritates them and can't help but remind them of what they've been through. Ideally this isn't our story or our children's reality. Let's do the digging now so once and for all healing can truly take place.

My scars indicate I've been hurt and chose to push through the pain. But that's not all. Scarred tissue is stronger than original flesh. It's hard to be hurt in the same way again once complete healing occurs. Isn't that a fabulous thing to think about? There's also little or no feeling on the scar itself.

Do you remember my story from chapter 1 about the rock that cut open my forehead? No scar remains. Time can make all evidence disappear. On the other hand, my longest knee scar is nine inches long and quite thick because of the deep cuts that were necessary. It will always be there. Of course, there's no pain. When I see the scar, I can choose what I remember. It could be the injuries that made surgery necessary, the very difficult recovery, or the fact that I'm healed, whole, and out of pain. What I think about is on me. My attitude makes the difference. Am I healthy? Reading the Word? Praying regarding my triggers?

CHILDREN WILL BE HURT

Wanting to avoid pain is normal. It's why we may cancel dentist appointments and not participate in extreme sports. You may look back on your life and remember emotional, social, physical, intellectual, or spiritual pain.

Wanting your children to experience less pain than you did or no pain at all makes sense. This is love, right? Less pain, yes. I would argue that expecting them to experience no pain isn't realistic, nor is it loving.

The culture can be confusing, we're imperfect, and children have free wills. Evil is present. Teach your children that disappointments, heartache, and pain are a part of life. This is loving, and ultimately protects them because they'll be discerning and choose to develop their inner resources. They'll look around to see what support they have available to them.

If you don't parent with this perspective, I fear children will be angry later when you're not there to protect them and they realize you didn't prepare them to handle challenges and to fail well. Young people have told me they felt lied to.

Pain

We can't avoid all pain. Emotional embarrassment, physical aches and pains, social putdowns, getting caught cheating on a major exam, rejection, even abuse are facts of life. I want your children to learn how to handle their emotions and reactions in the safety of your home.

Children who believe you don't want them to struggle may hide their pain from you. This may begin with your son not telling you about a peer on the playground who pushed him down and culminate in him not telling you about getting his girlfriend pregnant. Perhaps your daughter won't tell you she has been abused. Now you can't help them.

What would you benefit from thinking about?

- If you feel that your parents didn't prepare you for reality, in what ways is this influencing how you relate to your children's pain?
- Can you think of times when your children were hurt and it was made worse because they didn't think it would happen? How could you talk with them about it?

77

- If you're concerned your children are hiding their pain from you, how could you bring this up in a helpful conversation so they won't do it anymore? Will you make any changes to how you relate that you should explain?

THEY WON'T BOUNCE BACK

I'm glad you're reading this book. Maybe you have chosen it because you recognized you were overprotecting your children. Maybe the evidence showed up as their fragile behavior, and you noticed they couldn't risk being wrong. Maybe they're not trying new things. Maybe their complaints of assignments being too complicated and pleas of "Do it for me, Mommy!" have awakened you to your responsibility to parent them for healthy dependence and independence.

Maybe you think some children can recover from being hurt, but yours won't. You picture yours staying down and being unable to bounce back, come back, or bounce forward. Maybe because of past hurt, you have evidence that they treat failure as final. Their wounds aren't healing. Scars aren't forming.

Is this how you feel? You can choose to believe the truths I share and implement new ideas. When you do, your children and you will change. In the future, they will respond differently to traumatic experiences. Beliefs and information can change you and them!

Beliefs and Behaviors

Beliefs and behaviors are connected. Let me challenge you to understand that it's unnecessary to totally buy in to all the new ideas before tossing the bubble wrap and letting kids struggle. Trying something new to see if it works is more mature than not giving it a chance.

Many people try a new food plan without evidence it will work for them. They eliminate this and that based on recommendations and maybe some test results. They want to change badly enough that they give something new a try.

Maybe you've tried physical therapy or exercises for a back issue. You didn't know if anything would help, but you were desperate enough that you tried. It might have been painful, and it took a while for the benefits to become obvious, but you kept at it. In the same way, I invite you to try this new approach to challenges.

New beliefs (e.g., *My son believes he can bounce back*) can cause new behavior (e.g., *My son is asking for help and is not so quickly defeated and depressed*). And, your new behavior (e.g., *I'll leave the room to pray while my son struggles rather than watching and worrying*) can cause new beliefs (e.g., *God loves my son and cares about his future. Trusting Him and my son makes me a good mom*). When success is obvious, beliefs will begin to change. Now you're empowered to keep at it. Changes are possible.

What would you benefit from thinking about?

- What childhood memories do you have about bouncing back? Were you encouraged to bounce back or did you view failure as final?
- Think of one issue one of your children is struggling with. What are some new beliefs you want him or her to embrace so healthy behavior will result? Or if it's easier to think of the behaviors first, do that.
- What new beliefs and behaviors are you willing to consider so your children will more readily choose to recover from challenges?

WHAT IF IT'S ALL ABOUT ME?

These three reasons for wanting to protect children probably overlap. You don't want your children to experience pain, you're not sure they'll bounce back and learn from the experience, and some of your past experiences are relevant.

Many parents have told me how hard it is to watch children struggle and suffer. You feel their pain. I get that. You're intertwined in some amazing ways. I wouldn't want you to *not* feel their pain. I just don't want that desire to get in the way of what's best. I can't imagine you do either.

I've written it before and I'll write it again—you need to be resilient and healthy in order for your kids to be. If you haven't processed past defeat and trauma, watching your children struggle can bring your issues to the surface. Do you need to forgive someone? Have a conversation? Process feelings? Get some counseling?[2]

Sometimes a conversation with your children can be a key to your growth. I'm not suggesting you use them as counselors. That wouldn't be appropriate. But do let them know how hard it is for you to experience their suffering. Let them know you are choosing sometimes to let them face the consequences of their own decisions because it can help them grow. It's not unloving if you don't rescue them from every consequence. The exact opposite is true! Let them know you're available and want to support them, and sometimes that means being present without changing things.

They may not see the value of studying, so they stop putting in the effort—until they earn a C. You could have reminded your daughter about the test. You had many times before and now you decided it was time for her to suffer the consequences of her choices. When she complains and tries to blame you, talk with her about her responsibility to mature. Explain that your role is to love with support and not to rescue her. That C is not evidence that you're a bad mom. It's evidence you're a good mom because you're thinking of her need for healthy independence as she ages.

I ache for you because I imagine you know you must let your children walk out of the struggle or one day they'll deal with what you're dealing with. The other part of you wants to fly down in your helicopter and rescue them. I pray insights in this book are helping you. (There are more to come!)

You Can Do This!

On a Facebook post about this issue, my friend Alice wrote: "My head completely understands that hard times can produce wonderful fruit. But my children live in my heart." Right! I love this sentiment. Let me say this to you: you can do hard things! You can prioritize your children's present and future. You can choose to love long and strong and make it not about you.

Being rested and emotionally well are also key. I often hear about how exhausting it is to watch children struggle. Supporting them as they process ramifications of their decisions and how others treated them isn't for the faint of heart.

Are you trying to be a perfect parent and you define that partly as not allowing your children to be wrong or to be wronged? Do you think it's your responsibility to make things easy for them because your reputation is on the line? Are you trying to control everything? Do you need to fix their messes so you're the hero?

Taking It to the Extreme

As an extreme example, I still remember how I felt when I learned about the mom who wanted to make sure her daughter made the high school cheerleading squad. She hired a hit man to kill the mom of a rival cheerleader.[3] She hoped this would distract the girl enough that she wouldn't cheer well or maybe she wouldn't even try out. It's a true story!

Can you relate to this mom's choice in any way? Maybe you discourage your daughter from trying out for a competitive soccer team for fear she won't make it or she will but the coach will demand a lot from her. Maybe your son has figured out you don't want him to memorize a longer speech than he's ever done before for an upcoming speech and debate meet.

If your children learn you don't believe in them from your words and actions, they won't risk and grow. Ten years later your son may be offered a promotion and think about it with the internal question of "Would Mom think I could do this?"

If your parents overprotected you, can you see it as unhealthy now and rise above it?

In many years, your daughter may struggle in her marriage or with parenting a strong-willed little girl, but not feel safe asking you for guidance. Even then she may feel she'd disappoint you. She thinks, *I'm my mother's daughter. I should be able to do this easily and well. I can't let her feel like a failure. It would kill her.*

You know deep down that God didn't give you children to meet your needs or perform for you. It's not their responsibility to make you look good. You already care about this issue or you wouldn't be reading this book.

How can you determine why this is your pattern?

- If your parents overprotected you, can you see it as unhealthy, forgive them, and rise above it now?
- If you've been embarrassed or hurt by your children, can you forgive them and yourself, if appropriate?
- If comparisons and competition have set in with others, could you talk with them and help each other parent with freedom instead of fear?

EMBRACE LIFE WITH CONFIDENCE

As I've shared already, for your children to be confident about life, they need to learn how to walk through challenges. They must learn how to work things out, relying on inner resources of character, optimism, joy, purpose, and more. They must recognize and humble themselves to rely on support. Parents need to be at the top of that list. This won't happen if they sense you can't handle their pain.

Every time you turn around, you can see trauma. So can your children. Shootings, domestic abuse, the economy, health issues, unrest, divorce, hunger, homelessness, loss, grief . . . the list goes on.

Because of the prevalence of dysfunction and twenty-four-hour-a-day availability of "news," your children are aware that life can be hard. It is hard. If you act like it's not, you may lose credibility and influence. That's not what you want.

Your children will embrace life when they're not afraid of it. Do you remember walking on sidewalks and thinking "don't step on the crack or you'll break your mother's back"? You had to look down and think of nothing else. Your thoughts were negative. You were fearful. (I realize it was a "game," but the hard emotions are there.) Great things could have passed you by and you wouldn't have known. This can be the mindset of you and your children if you stay in a "yes, but . . ." relationship to children's trauma.

Seeds grow in darkness.

But he was pierced for our transgressions; he was crushed
for our iniquities; upon him was the chastisement that brought us
peace, and with his wounds we are healed.
Isaiah 53:5

What to Do:
CONVERSATIONS That
Build RESILIENCY

Everything we do at Celebrate Kids relates to our five core needs
that must be met.[1] Children can embrace life when they are
secure, like their *identity*, have solid *belonging*, are *purposeful*, and
competent. They'll be determined and more likely to want to be
well and do well. They'll be equipped to avoid some trauma and
learn from what they encounter. They'll be resilient!

When these needs aren't met, depression, confusion, and anger
can grip your children. Resiliency will be the furthest thing from
their mind. They won't believe they can bounce back and they
won't know why they'd bother trying.

Think about your children's resiliency as you read these
descriptions:

Security—Who can I trust? If your children can't trust you, they won't admit when they're struggling, tell you about past trauma, or ask you for help, especially regarding "big T" trauma. When they can trust you, you become a voice of truth to them.

Identity—Who am I? If your children only know their weaknesses, believe lies about themselves, and don't work to overcome challenges and heartache, they won't become who God created them to be. When they care what you think about them and they know they can believe you, you become their dictionary.

Belonging—Who wants me? If your children don't want to be with you or be known as your children, they won't expect you to support them or care if you do. Offering help will be hard for you. When they want you and want to be wanted by you, you become their safe healing place.

Purpose—Why am I alive? If your children don't know why they're alive and they have no healthy goals to fulfill, they may think suffering is their plight in life. They may expect bad things to happen so they don't bother telling you when they do. When you influence their beliefs about why God made them, they'll want to bounce back and go beyond where they were. Now you have become a source of hope for them.

Competence—What do I do well? Without the first four needs met, healthy competence is impossible. Children won't believe they can grow or change. They won't have reasons to apply themselves and they won't think they can rely on you to motivate or teach them how. They'll believe they have no strengths to rely on and no one to trust with their questions. Being resilient is nearly impossible. When you teach them how to bounce back, make healthy decisions, and develop mature character, they can be competent. Now you are their coach.

Did you see your children in these descriptions? Maybe yourself? By being a voice of truth, their dictionary, safe healing place, a source of hope, and their coach, you provide profound support and give them inner resources. It sounds like a lot, but don't be overwhelmed. You can meet these needs through presence, talking, and listening. Truly!

Intentional Connection

To meet your children's core needs and to grow their resiliency, you'll need to do what you do when you want anything to change. Be intentional in what you say and don't say, what you do and don't do, and how much time you make and take for the issue.

Your intentionality can create healthy connections. Your bond empowers children to "withstand and learn from difficult and traumatic experiences."[2] That's what you want—that your children will recognize and resist all trauma possible and learn from whatever challenges they must navigate.

Talking regularly will help children avoid trauma. Their need for belonging is being met at home and because of your influence,

89

they're bound to think better of themselves. This helps them avoid dysfunction, bullying, and more. They'll want to avoid pain and stand up after falling down. They'll know how because of your role modeling and teaching as you hang out together. The expectation to constantly connect makes it easier for children to bounce back, come back, and bounce forward.

Please Remember

Don't feel any shame if you've not used the ideas I explain below or if you've tried some and haven't been successful. You can choose to use them now and hopefully my approach will facilitate your success. The important thing is, you are reading this now to learn new ideas.

Talking regularly will help children avoid trauma.

This, of course, is true for all I've written in the book, but I felt I should share this now. I pray that my work will always add to your hope and empower you to courageously try new ideas more than once if they don't initially result in the changes I've predicted.

HOW TO ENCOURAGE HONEST CONVERSATIONS

You can teach a lot through timely and strategic conversations, so be alert to opportunities and be willing to take the time. Because kids won't have their guard up like they might when they're expecting a lecture, you'll get through to them with more truth. These conversations build trust—when they're done well. Trust and truth are the bedrock of resiliency.

Have Ongoing Conversations, Not One Discussion

Regular conversations about tough stuff need to happen if you want your children to grow in resiliency. But, in addition, work to always be talking about the basics of resiliency. Are you all still defining mistakes as things done incorrectly? They're no big, ugly deal. Are you remembering that failure is falling short of an expectation and not taking advantage of the opportunity to learn from mistakes? It's not final or fatal. Make sure your children use these words correctly when talking about their days and experiences.

Keep the words "resilient" and "resiliency" in use. Keep talking about the mindset, beliefs, and process we need to be resilient. Talk about the choices that resilient people make and the goal that resiliency become a part of everyone's character.

After a discussion about a challenging situation or trauma is over, being relieved is understandable. Hopefully peace will reign for a while. But, children may have new, related experiences that cause questions to come up about the issue you just discussed. Or, as they mature, they may have new questions about former conversations. It's also possible that nothing changes, and they just need to be comforted and reassured. You don't want them to be alone with their concerns, fearful you'll be upset with them if they bring up the issue again. Being open to ongoing conversations is healthiest.

In addition, you're bound to learn more about the issues you and your son or daughter talked about. You'll want to bring up your ideas without them complaining, "We already talked about that!" Therefore, let them know you expect to have regular conversations.

When you and your children know anyone can revisit a topic and past pain, it's easier for them to come to you when it's again on their mind. And it makes it easier for you to bring up the topic again without them pushing back.

Lead, Don't Ask

You might be thinking, *Kathy, that makes sense, but I can't get my kids to talk to me!* All parents have been frustrated by getting grunts instead of answers when asking children questions. Children are more likely to answer you and provide helpful information when they know you're listening to understand and not to analyze or judge them. Acknowledging their pain rather than dismissing it also helps them trust you. Now they can be honest.

When your children stop talking for a minute, leading statements can be more effective than follow-up questions. When you ask things like, "What did you do next?" and "Who else was there?" and "Why did they pick on you?" you force children to go to a part of the story they may not have planned to share next. And your tone of voice can indicate judgment, anger, fear, and disappointment that shut your children down.

"Tell Me More"

When your children stop talking for a bit, with a leading tone of voice, say "Keep talking . . ." If they respond "What??" with a snarky attitude, respond calmly with "Help me understand," or "Keep sharing." Then wait. Silence is a powerful invitation to talk. "I have time now" is another honoring thing to say.

Wear your "parent face" and try not to show emotional responses as you listen. This keeps your children talking. They may stop sharing if you show disappointment, fear, or anger too soon. Or they may change the story and lie because keeping you happy is important to them.

Be Fully Present without Your Phone

Another thing that can help children communicate well is to put your phone away when you want to talk. Your children will feel important and that can change their attitudes.

My friend Sally set a wise policy for her sons. She immediately hung up if she was on the phone when they came home from school. The first thirty minutes were theirs. They enjoyed a snack and talked about their day. Then they'd get busy playing or doing homework and Sally could call her friend back. Her sons felt honored and took advantage of the time. Your children may do the same.

Children hesitate to begin a difficult conversation if they predict they'll have to start over. I'm the same way and I bet you are too. They've had enough experience to know if you hear your phone ting or ring you'll be distracted. Therefore, they don't share, and you miss the chance to learn what's going on. You may not discover whether they've experienced trauma lately or are falling into depression. At least silence your phone (and tell them you have). Or leave it behind when you visit in the bedroom or go for a walk.

Just You and Your Child

Talking at the dinner table may seem like an old-fashioned recommendation, but families truly benefit when eating dinner together.[3] It's not just about the food, it's about the conversations. Sharing about your days connects you. It can be effective for each of you to share a highlight and lowlight. You can be curious and supportive of each other.

But to expect children to open up and provide lots of details and be vulnerable with siblings around the dinner table is asking a lot. It's not surprising that one of my vivid childhood memories is choosing to talk with my mom in my parents' bedroom about something difficult. My brother and I got along well and I loved my dad, but I must have known I needed more privacy to go deep.

This is why taking children out one at a time to their favorite places is so wise. Some dads do one Saturday a month with different children. A mom can go for a walk around the block with one child at a time on different nights. Ask them to elaborate about recently shared highlights and lowlights. Don't get into the habit of only talking about negative things. They'll be more willing to join you and be fully present to your curiosity and concerns if they know they'll also get to talk about good things. Your children may never say thank you. Do it anyway.

> *When children don't have to look at you, it's easier for them to be honest and transparent.*

Rethinking Eye Contact

Eye contact can be a sign of respect, so we tend to expect it and ask for it when talking with children and listening to them. Yet when children don't have to look at you, it's easier for them to be honest, detailed, vulnerable, and transparent. Children tell me they don't like looking into your eyes when they'll disappoint you. They don't want to remember your "mad face." This is true when you talk and when you listen. Therefore, especially when needing to talk about difficult circumstances, I recommend strategies that don't require eye contact.

The Dark Is Inviting

Try talking in the dark. You might have discovered that bedtime can be a rich time to find out what's happened. You can wait at the door after putting your children to bed, hang out by the door when older kids put themselves to bed, and even lie down with them for prayers or to share with them and wait for them to open up.

Don't end on a difficult note, though. You want sleep to be pleasant, so pray about tough stuff, change the subject at the end, or tell your children a story. Do something that won't make them feel like you're dismissing the value of what you just accomplished, but that leaves them in a good place emotionally.

Car Talks

Children are more likely to open up in the car when it's digital-free.[4] They like that you can't make extended eye contact with them. The fact that you're both captured means more details can be shared and no one can leave if conversations get difficult. (Remember, though, that if siblings are present chances are good that no one will be very vulnerable.)

Get Busy

Boys especially like talking when they're busy doing something with you. They can help you clean out the garage, deliver food to church shut-ins, walk the aisles of a home repair store, or enjoy playing a game. If you don't force it, many boys will simply start talking in these side-by-side or shoulder-to-shoulder experiences that make eye contact less necessary. They have a lot to say. Spend time with them and wait.

Pillow Journals

Especially for girls, pillow journals can work to get more information about negative experiences you wonder if your daughter has experienced. Write her a note and leave it on her pillow. It may be easier for her to read your thoughts, concerns, and questions without immediately responding like she would have to do during a conversation. And she may pour her heart out to you and ask questions as she writes back because you can't immediately ask her for more information or react in fear to what she tells you. The written conversation should eventually lead to a face-to-face conversation.

EMBRACE LIFE WITH CONFIDENCE

I was driving east on a street I am regularly on when I realized the speed bump wasn't in front of me. I was preparing to brake for it as I've done for years. The cement in front of me was flat! I was able to continue on at the typical speed. The city must have made the change when I was out of town because I had no idea.

It took me many days of driving to remember the speed bump

was not there. My habit was so ingrained that I frequently took my foot off the gas pedal to slow down and then get ready to brake as I approached that area. I eventually remembered I didn't need to.

I think it might be similar for parents and children who are used to negative conversations, interrogations, or lectures. Maybe there have been grunts for answers and arguing instead of communicating, followed by pouting and silence or one or more of you leaving the room.

Because it's been the norm, it's what you may expect to happen again when you speak or hear those frightening words "Let's talk!" But then you commit to growing. You discuss changes you all agree to work on. You learn strategies and become equipped. But because of habits and hurts, parents and children might still expect the negative so you all put on the brakes. With each positive conversation, hope will rise, and you can keep moving.

You should not expect instant change in your children or yourself, but do expect change to eventually happen. You must be compassionate and patient. You must be resilient and keep trying even when old patterns want to crowd back in. Talking and listening. What profoundly important reasons to be resilient! You're all worth the effort!

Grapes need to be crushed to make wine.

Trust in him at all times, O people; pour out your heart
before him; God is a refuge for us.

Psalm 62:8

What to Say:
CONVERSATIONS That
Build RESILIENCY

Now that you've learned some new ideas about having healthy conversations, let's turn our attention to the content of those discussions. Since we're specifically looking at building resiliency, you'll be talking about mistakes, failure, trauma, effort, disappointments, struggles, forgiveness, emotions, and the like.

Being available and ready will serve your children well. They might wish their lives had reboot buttons so they can just pretend hard things don't happen, but that's not reality. Hard things happen, messy people sin, and we disappoint ourselves. Processing all of this makes it less likely they'll be snared again in similar ways. Your input is significant.

As an author, I greatly appreciate the undo button in the upper left corner of my laptop as I type this sentence. I can delete something, change my mind, and get it right back. I can add a sentence, realize it doesn't add anything valuable, and quickly delete it. One click. Done. Changing life's circumstances isn't nearly as easy.

Because technology masquerades as being perfect, and it profoundly influences your children's minds and hearts, they may believe their lives should be perfect. This may be among the reasons they're more frustrated when things don't go their way than you think is appropriate. Their tools, toys, programs, and apps have taught them that they can one-click away the junk.

Your consistent, faithful, on-their-side availability to listen and talk will settle your children. This is the scaffolding they need. It's how your foundation becomes solid and you establish your role as a strategist. You become their model of how to live life realistically and well—a valued source of truth, their coach, their dictionary, their safe healing place, their hope.

YOUR WORDS

I imagine you can think of times when your reactions to your children's struggles and pain were helpful and when they weren't. Our words can ease emotional pain or add to their hurt. Our words can even prevent problems from occurring in the first place.

Communicating truths about all five core needs, as we've already discussed, will help to secure your children's hearts. Now resilience is much more likely. Your children will be willing to admit they need you. They'll handle loss without whining and not allow themselves to be defined by what's happened to them.

Also, tell children when they're being resilient. Define the word for them. Remember, identity controls behavior. Your comments will help the positive behaviors continue.

For example, rather than saying your daughter is "good," tell her you're glad she was "brave to try again because resilience makes you stronger." Tell your son, "Not giving up on yourself or blaming others for things that are your responsibility are mature qualities of resiliency. I'm proud of you."

What other truths do you believe you should strategically and regularly communicate to build resiliency? Allow me to recommend this family resiliency manifesto:

Our Family's Resiliency Manifesto

We understand struggling is sometimes necessary. We will not hide our challenges from each other. We expect to learn from the experience and make progress.

We will remember that we sometimes struggle because not all learning is easy, the culture is chaotic, people are messy, and much of life isn't fair. Our challenges are not always our fault.

We will not panic when we make mistakes. But if we feel like we are, we'll let someone help us.

We will not rescue each other too soon, but we will if necessary.

We will not give up on ourselves or on one another.

We will work to prevent trauma and help one another recover from what pain they do experience.

We will not expect each other to immediately get over their feelings and quickly trust again after they've been hurt. We will be patient and helpful.

We expect our attitudes to be positive and our character to grow.

We will help each other grow by teaching, supporting, and expecting as much as we think is possible.

We will be a significant source of each other's security, identity, belonging, purpose, and competence.

We will always point to God as the authentic One who meets our needs through who He is and what He does.

We will teach each other about God's purposes for the challenges He allows us to experience.

We will teach that God believes in us and He won't give up on us. He may not always give us what we want or need when we think it's best. This doesn't mean He doesn't love us. He might say no because He does love us.[1]

I'm certainly not recommending lectures about each point. Instead, take advantage of teachable moments. Show your children you're alert and engage them in spontaneous conversations. You can also plan conversations as you see needs arise. You can grow children's resiliency simply by responding to their feelings and reactions and talking and listening! Think about whether your communication reinforces the Manifesto or not. Then be resilient and make changes if you need to.

TO FEEL THEIR PAIN, LISTEN AND OBSERVE

You might want to talk with your kids to answer their questions, solve their problems, and fix their situations. This is understandable. But if you don't first acknowledge their pain, confusion, and doubts, many children won't care what you say about their situation. They'll feel analyzed rather than loved. They'll feel like problems you're trying to solve and projects you're trying to finish if you don't start with their emotions. They'll feel like they are the problem rather than children with a problem.[2]

Of course, listen to their words, but not just to know what they think. You want to know what they feel. Listen to *how* they say what they say. Are they confident? Hesitant? Angry? Hopeless?

Also, learn to listen for what your children don't say. What didn't your children elaborate on that seemed important to you? What details seemed very important to them? I imagine all of us could listen more carefully and longer.[3] What they say and don't say will tell you much about what they need from you.

Consider Each Child

Acknowledging frustration, fear, anger, and pain looks different for every child. As I explain below, asking what's wrong usually isn't helpful. You can privately say, "I acknowledge your pain. I'm here with you."[4] I love the word "with." A lot of people would say, "I'm here for you." "For" implies your interest is to help them. Connecting makes the difference!

Learn to listen for what your children don't say.

You don't have to have all the answers! Be present. Be willing to "weep with those who weep."[5]

Especially with boys, you won't want to get overly emotional. They may not know how to respond to your emotions. But, feel their pain—don't dismiss or ignore it. See it, hear it, and mention it. What happened to them and how they're responding may make you uncomfortable. You may want to express your sadness and anger. Be alert so you can discern what's appropriate.

Get Specific

As you become aware of your children's frustration and pain, help them label negative emotions specifically so they're easier to deal with.[6] For instance, "I feel sad" is general, but "I'm feeling lonely" is more specific. Many things can result in sadness. It helps you to know whether your daughter is lonely, disappointed, jealous, or confused.

"I'm feeling frustrated that we lost again after having such a big lead!" is more specific and helpful than "I'm mad!" By putting feelings into words, children have more power over their emotions. Now your help will be more strategic when it is appropriate to start problem solving.

Feel and Feeling

Also, notice the words "feeling" and "feel" in the above examples. These words make the statements temporary. Your son or daughter currently feels lonely, but it doesn't mean loneliness will continue. Using the word "am," as in "I am lonely," makes the statement sound like it's a permanent part of your daughter's identity. This can worsen a sense of hopelessness and make bouncing back more unlikely.

You can model this by using "feel" and "feeling" when you share about your own feelings. For example, "I'm feeling disappointed about your choice" and "I'm feeling so confused that you lied." When you think they're ready to understand, carefully suggest your children use new wording. They may not immediately understand the significance. That's okay. You get it and that's enough. Your reactions and brief explanations will help them grow.

You don't want your corrections to come across as dismissals of their feelings. Statements like "Why are you so sad again?" and "Just get over it!" don't help. You want your children to use their feelings. They're a natural consequence that will help your children make healthy changes.[7]

DON'T ASK "WHAT'S WRONG?"

While you're becoming aware of your children's feelings, it's easy to ask, "What's wrong?" or "How are you feeling?" or "Are you okay?" Yet these questions are often ineffective, especially with boys. They may not have a robust emotional vocabulary.[8]

You might also ask questions like, "Are you depressed?" and "Why are you so anxious?" and "Why are you angry all the time?" These questions, and others like them, are also not easy for children to answer. Children may not know why they're anxious or angry. They don't know what depression feels like. I don't always know, and I've had many more experiences than they have. Unfortunately, now you've added to their stress. And, because they're aware that depression isn't a good thing, now they're upset that you're stressed. (But I get it—you're asking with great motives.)

Do Talk about What You Observe

Even if I can't identify an emotion driving my behavior, I can recognize how I behave. Your kids can too. Teaching them to self-evaluate to be aware of themselves, their choices, and their actions is essential.

For me, impatience and a critical spirit are the first signs that something is wrong. When I realize I'm behaving in these ways, I slow down, pray, reflect, and self-evaluate to determine why. Then I may realize I haven't forgiven someone and bitterness is taking over. Sometimes it's that I've blown something way out of proportion. My explanatory style shows up—I'm sure *everyone* is aware that I disappointed someone. You get the idea.

This is why I recommend you tell children what you've noticed that has you concerned, rather than asking about their emotions. You can find out what's going on and what's happened. You have to get there through a back door of sorts. It might sound like this:

> "Jake, normally you're very kind and patient when teaching Alan a new game. Today you weren't. What's up?"

> "Carly, the last few nights you haven't wanted to help me prepare dinner. I've missed your help and our laughter. I get the sense you're avoiding me. Have I hurt you or is there something else going on?"

> "Kids, we've noticed you're not as excited about going to youth group as in the past. Is there anything we should know? Has something happened to change your attitude? Can we help in any way?"

LISTEN FOR UNHEALTHY THINKING

As your children share what happened and tell you their stories, listen for cognitive distortions[9] and extreme thinking.[10] They can be signs of depression and pessimistic explanatory styles. Children might overgeneralize and frequently use words like "never" and "always." They might negate the positive, amplify the negative, and blow things out of proportion. These thinking patterns are a sure detriment to resiliency.

Many children with little or no hope don't think about bouncing back and changing. They often just work to get comfortable in their valley. You'll want to correct their thinking. You need to. Therefore, listen intently and observe what's been going on. Give them a new, accurate script for their self-talk. For example:

Child Says	You Say
"I'll never get it right!"	"I know you're discouraged. This is only the third day you've worked on this piece for your piano teacher. It's not fair to you or her to give up. Remember you did great with last week's song because you stayed positive. I was proud of you. Based on last week's experience, I think you'll improve today. How can I help you? I have time now. And, what's an accurate way to express your concerns?"
"I'll always be embarrassed!"	"I know it feels that way now and it's frustrating and scary. I don't like being embarrassed either. I'm so sorry. You're old enough to know that the kids will move on and think about something or someone else pretty soon so this is not true. You need to speak truth to yourself. How could you reword this as truth? And could I help you plan something fun to talk about or do on Sunday when you're with this group again? What are you confident about? You could give them something new to think about!"
"It's all my fault!"	"That's not true and you know it. We need you to speak the truth to yourself. I know you're sad and upset. Your brother has already apologized for his attitude. I admitted I could have been more organized so you wouldn't have had to wait. And we talked about how we'll help you develop self-control. You were responsible for part of the problem and not all of it. How could you reword your statement as truth? Do you want to work on anything related to the problem now? How can I help you?"

TALK TO BE UNDERSTOOD

Your instruction will be believed and understood when you pay attention to what your children say and don't say and how they feel. Now you'll be able to nuance your instruction and the examples to help you make your points. Your input will be meaningful and relevant.

Remember, don't make listening to solve problems your primary goal. And don't listen for your turn to talk. Listen to understand. Your children will notice and they'll trust you more. Their emotional safety should be a high goal.

Share Your Evidence

When you do share instructions about how your children can handle themselves going forward, use phrases like "I've noticed . . ." and "I know because . . ." Evidence doesn't lie. I've taught this principle for years when we compliment and correct children.[11] Now you can use the phrase when instructing your children. It will help them understand you, believe you, and act on your input. For example:

> "Let's make sure to have a slower, calmer day before your next competition. This means you'll have time to practice when you want to. I know this will help because I've noticed that you perform better after days like this. You're more focused and rested so you can concentrate. Does this make sense?"

> "I think it will help to distance yourself from Sarah. I've noticed that your depression began when you started hanging out with her more. Look at the calendar with me. Remember your schedule and the parties? You've told me that she's competitive and compares herself to everyone else to feel better about herself. You've been doing that. Do you remember what you said

an hour or so ago? Would you be willing to take at least a week off from seeing her, and we'll pay attention to how you feel? How can I help you say no the next time she invites you to get together?"

Let Your Children Be the Heroes

Your insights and instruction matter greatly. You're a definite source of hope and healing for your children. Yet providing the right input to prevent or solve problems can't be your primary goal. That might surprise you.

Parent so your children become their own heroes. Be a sounding board to help them learn to think and feel right about what happened. Guide them to know what they can do next and what they shouldn't do. When children make their own decisions, they're more likely to act on their ideas, follow through, and use the successful ones again in the future.[12] Their confidence and appropriate independence are among their most critical inner resources they can now rely on in the future.

BE AWARE OF YOUR WORDS' POWER

I began this chapter with a suggested Resiliency Manifesto—truths to believe and communicate that will help your children become more resilient. Let me close the chapter with additional insights about the substance of your conversations.

Be alert to how you respond to your children's frustrations. Not only can your reactions and comments crash a conversation, but your words can also set children on a path of life or death.[13]

How you respond to children's emotions, stories, and questions can encourage resiliency or perfectionism and fear. Ginsburg's insight is so important: "In routine daily conversations, we drop clues that we're judging, moralizing, minimizing, negating, catastrophizing, belittling, and shaming."[14] You usually don't mean to, but you may!

James's Story

Friends of mine thought about scheduling an elective cosmetic surgery for their son. They were concerned that peers might especially tease James as he got older. Imagine James arriving home from school. As his lowlight after dinner, he shared privately with his parents that he was teased. Then, as tears formed in his eyes, he bravely added that his teacher said he'll always be teased and he just needs to grow up and handle it.[15]

Undermine Their Confidence

If the mom asks, "What does she know?" she undermines James's confidence in his teacher, someone his parents have taught him to respect. He also won't feel supported by his mom because her question isn't helpful.

Child Loses Respect

If his dad reacts, "That's ridiculous! You're not always going to be teased!" James will see that his dad isn't taking the problem seriously and he called his teacher a liar. James may also lose respect for his dad because it appears he doesn't understand the reality of his school experiences.

Confuses the Child

If his mom announces, "Your teacher had no right to say that!" she creates a moral judgment for James. He is supposed to be able to trust his teacher, and he thought she and his parents were all on his side. Now he doesn't know what to think.

Catastrophizes the Problem

A mom or dad can turn the problem into a catastrophe by proclaiming, "Okay! We'll never let you leave the house again!" This overstatement, which isn't realistic, just confuses James. Now he might think his appearance and the teasing actually are big deals. He had been trying to believe his parents, that it wouldn't be "that bad," but now he doesn't know what to think.

Minimizes the Problem

The opposite can happen. James's dad can minimize the problem by dismissing James's emotions with, "It's not that bad. I've seen worse!" This too can alarm James. He might feel his dad can't handle him and doesn't believe it's hard. He won't feel seen or understood.

Compares Unnecessarily

We need to avoid comparisons, too, which Lori Wildenberg identifies as hope killers.[16] His dad already did this when sharing "I've seen worse." Other comparisons can sound like this: "Others wouldn't think it's a big deal at all," "I had my own stuff to deal with when I was your age," and "At least you can run fast."

What Can You Do Instead?

Are you wondering what to do instead? Not saying anything isn't an option. As I've written, though, you can listen longer before you speak. You can learn to slow down and not blurt out ideas without considering your children.

Feel Their Pain

Remember to feel your children's pain before trying to solve their problems. Acknowledge it. Sometimes the best thing to do is to hold them tight. Let them cry and cry with them. Wait for them to relax before talking.

Saying "I'm sorry" is powerful and always will be. You can elaborate if it's wise. "I'm sorry this happened to you," "I'm sorry you're in pain."

When the time is right to learn more, maybe start with the leading statement ideas. Listen to understand what happened and also to learn more about the condition

Saying "I'm sorry" is powerful and always will be.

of your child's heart and mind. "And . . . ," "Tell me more so I understand . . . ," "What else would you like me to know?"

When children talk about their feelings, remember to do your best to help them get specific. But be careful because you won't want them to shut down if they feel like they're doing something wrong. Judgment can do that. You can wait to talk about this later. Specifics help them process accurately which helps them heal and become resilient, so do talk about it.

Take Appropriate Responsibility

Apologize if you realize what you said might have come across differently from what you intended. Explain what you meant. Explain what you didn't mean. Talk about a different way you could have communicated your frustration, fear, or anger. Or just say that you're sorry your words added to their pain, frustration, or anxiety.

Indeed, if your children think you're responsible in any way for the mess they're in, acknowledge that. Tell them you're sorry without including excuses. For example, "I realize if I would have been on time, you wouldn't have gotten stressed and acted the way you did."

Notice what I wrote. The key is if *they think* you're responsible. You may not think you are, but to help them trust you and increase resilience, if there's anything true about this, acknowledge it. Later, when emotions are calmer, you can talk about their need for self-control, patience, and putting others first. To develop a healthier explanatory style that can change everything, they need to learn not to blame others when things go wrong so it is wise for you to talk about this in the right way at the right time.

My guess is that when your children apologize for something, you don't like for them to make excuses. It might sound like this: "Yes, Mom, I was late, but Bethany needed my help with something and then I realized I forgot to give Mr. Jake the new piano music so I had to stop there." You might even interrupt by declaring, "There's no excuse! Just learn to be on time!"

If you make excuses for yourself and your behavior, they'll see the hypocrisy. They'll be disappointed, confused, and possibly angry. They may choose not to even come to you in the future to talk about their trauma experience. This diminishes security and trust, the first core need that must be met to establish healthy relationships.

Do things sometimes happen that cause us to run late? Absolutely! Are there causes for impatience, fear, jealousy, resentment, and more? Of course. We don't want reasons to become excuses for our choices and behavior. We want to be led by our beliefs—people are more important than things, and I can do what I need to do. Let's model and talk about this.

Be an Advocate

You need to hear your children's hearts, consider past reactions and conversations, and speak up as an advocate. Perhaps call teachers, coaches, and parents of friends and make sure your children know you did. Depending on what's happened, have them sit with you. Tell the person you call why you're calling and explain that you'd like to put them on speaker so your child can listen. Ask permission.

Help your children talk directly to peers and adults when they can. You can help them decide how to begin the conversation, suggest a few statements and questions to use, and practice a conversation. If they won't talk with a peer and you believe you should, talk with your children about why you think it's essential and what you'll communicate.

What You Won't Want to Do

James's parents shouldn't ask, "Were you teased?" every time he comes home from school or church. They won't want James to think that his appearance or potential teasing are their focus. Certainly, if he talks about it again as his lowlight of the day, or they sense it might have happened, they'll want to appropriately follow through, most likely without siblings around.

Make sure to talk about other things. Start with strengths and fun things. Always talk about character. "What made you laugh today?" "Did you help anyone today? How did that make you and them feel?" "Where did you shine today?" "What's one of the hardest things you did today? How did you handle it?"

Among the most important things to ask is, "How can we help you?" This is better than "Can we help?" It might be even better to ask, "How can we help you now?" If your children respond with grunts, but you sense they need you, you can try a multiple-choice option. "Would you like to be left alone, go for a walk together, tell me more in fifteen minutes, or pray together?" Sometimes they'll indicate their preference with a shift in eye contact and not words, so watch for that. And, if you know a scoop of ice cream would make them feel seen, head to the freezer and dish it up.

Being your children's support and teaching them beliefs and strategies they can use to hold their heads high will make them resilient. They'll be more confident in how God made them and less of a target for their friends.

EMBRACE LIFE WITH CONFIDENCE

Did you notice what I never recommended in this chapter? I never recommended you share advice, suggestions, or opinions with your children. I did recommend you share instruction. That's because suggestions, advice, and opinions are harder to obey. In fact, children assume they don't have to obey them or follow through.

The Old Testament book of Esther recounts how Esther, a young woman, became queen of Persia and saved the Jewish people.[17] Her cousin, Mordecai, is one of my Bible heroes because he stepped in to raise her when he didn't have to.

Mordecai didn't just raise Esther. He raised her well. In Esther 2 we read that Esther "continued to follow Mordecai's instructions as she had done when he was bringing her up" (v. 20 NIV). Throughout the book we read of her courage and obedience. Mordecai was able to ask much of Esther partly because he knew he had instructed her. He taught her. He didn't offer her suggestions, opinions, and advice. These are easier to doubt and question. He was confident in Esther, how he had influenced her, and most importantly, in the God in her. I want you to be confident in the same ways. You'll be able to truly prepare your children for great opportunities God presents to them.

"Fall down seven times, get up eight." —Japanese proverb[18]

". . . who knows whether you have not come
to the kingdom for such a time as this?"
Esther 4:14

Get Unstuck: Moving from SETBACK to COMEBACK

Maybe you were motivated to read this book because your children have avoided hard things. They haven't valued effort and have been afraid to make mistakes. Or maybe they have been in the habit of giving up when challenged or hurt. You recognized they were fragile and not growing as much as they could be.

Maybe your son has experienced enough trauma that depression has set in. Maybe you began to recognize his pessimistic mindset. He, therefore, has made little progress because he blamed himself for everything that went wrong and believed nothing would ever change.

I truly pray the book has been helpful and you believe changes can happen. I imagine some of your beliefs have already changed and you're successfully implementing some new strategies. Good for you!

GROWTH HAPPENS

Your children will learn to trust you as you encourage and support them more. If they're used to you bubble-wrapping them or hovering over them, they received several messages: they can't take care of themselves; you don't trust them to be all right or do all right; it's your job to protect them; and challenges are terrible. No wonder they're stuck—unsure of themselves, treading water to avoid moving forward into darkness, or sitting down in the valleys they find themselves in.

Your new beliefs about mistakes, struggles, and the benefits of challenges will cause you to react differently to your children's "little t" and "big T" trauma. You want them to believe they'll benefit from walking through hard times so they don't want to avoid them anymore. This will take time.

At first your children are bound to be confused. They may question you and push back because they're fearful. They wonder if they can trust you. They will become more courageous. Watch for this character quality to show up as they engage in challenges, vulnerably process frustrations, and ask for help and follow through.

Be patient and don't give up on yourself, them, or these ideas even on hard days. You can all change. Growth happens.

Independence Is Necessary

My brother, Dave, and his wife, Debbie, have three children who are now married young adults. It's not hard for me to remember many great times with them at neighborhood parks when they were little. Watching them swinging is a favorite memory. I can still see the delight on their faces and hear their giggles.

They didn't start out swinging on their own. Debbie, Dave, or I had to lift them onto the swing. If we didn't immediately start pushing them, they became frustrated. They were stuck unless we pushed them. They didn't know how to move by pumping their legs so they were totally dependent on one of us.

We pushed and laughed with them as they went higher and higher. Eventually, Betsy, Katie, and Andy moved their legs but didn't get any power from them at first. Then, with age, growing strength, and experience, they pumped and swung higher and higher.

They didn't need us anymore. We didn't teach them what to do. They figured it out.

Andy, Katie, and Betsy loved their independence. Discovering they were capable and didn't need us to get started or keep going made them happy. If we had kept pushing, needing to be in control, they would have complained and most likely lost interest in swinging. Of course, we didn't abandon them. They didn't go to the park alone for a long time, and they didn't swing without someone keeping an eye on them.

Perhaps your children have been stuck for a while. They may be gripped by fear, doubt, or past negative experiences. Unforgiveness, shame, or confusion may rule their hearts.

Your children may be more willing to work on changing now that you believe new things and will parent differently. As they watch you, they can learn how to "pump" independently. In addition to all you've learned about guiding your children during struggles, these ideas can get them unstuck. This is essential or hope will evaporate and dreams will die.

BE PRESENT

In chapter 6, I wrote about being fully present without your phone so conversations can be rich. The concept of being present is worth expanding.

One of the best ways to be for your children is to be with them.

For your children to want you to be present, you'll need to pay attention to them and talk about what they're doing right and what they could improve. Talking about strengths encourages them. You'll be pointing out inner resources they can rely on to avoid trauma, overcome weaknesses, and handle disappointments, frustrations, and hurt.

Be with Your Children

One of the best ways to be *for* your children is to be *with* them. Your availability and attention communicate that you're on their side. Sometimes you may guide them, side by side. Sometimes you may go ahead of them to take the lead. Your role may be to gently push them from behind because you know what they're capable of. These "with positions" are only possible when you choose to be fully present.

Putting your children first and being engaged with them in these ways allows you to see what's going on in real time. What or who frustrates them? Is their attitude the problem? What's overwhelming them? When did the pessimism first show up? Where is the fear coming from?

Learn What Can Be Controlled

One of the greatest gifts you'll give your children is a reality check about what they can control. Being present to see how they do what they do and what you hear them blame when things don't go well will guide your conversations.

Children will not be healthy or resilient if they believe negative qualities about themselves or think situations are permanent when they're not. They'll believe that being stuck is their permanent condition. Effort, diligence, initiative, and hope won't matter.

Maybe you hear your daughter mutter under her breath, *They hate me! They'll always hate me!* After acknowledging her feelings, you can carefully ask about what happened and hang out in the back of the room next time to notice how the group she's a part of interacts. You may see that your daughter always draws attention back to herself after others have talked. Rather than asking her friends questions or sharing feelings about what they shared, she typically responds with, *That makes me think of a time when I . . .* You'll equip her to know how to change when you explain the danger of this self-centered approach to conversations, share examples of what she did, and talk about how it would make her friends feel. She can control more about her relationships than she thinks.

Direct Communication

You don't want children to give up when they can do things to get themselves unstuck. They just need to know what will help. This is when your direct communication is essential. It's bound to be relevant and beneficial if you've been fully present to your children.

Maybe you notice your son berating himself with, *I'll always be the slowest. It's so embarrassing!* You can help him compare his performances to his former self and not to others. Keep old work and show him there are more problems on a page than two weeks ago. He's not slower, and might even be quicker. You could time him on his math work. Encourage him to state this accurately and ask if he wants your help to improve.

If your son is slow and may remain among the slowest in his class, don't lie or exaggerate his ability to change. You need to help him change his goals, accept his limitations, and celebrate his strengths. You can help him stop comparing himself unfairly to others. He may still look stuck because he's not improving, but he won't be emotionally stuck and frustrated trying to change something that can't improve.

Anxiety and Control

Anxiety results from not knowing what we can and can't control.[1] There are other causes, but think about this in light of your anxiety and your children's. It's likely to be an important factor. Talk with them about this. A calm assurance can happen when children know what's permanent and what isn't. What can they influence and what can't they?

At first, the reality of how much can't change may be devastating. Making time to grieve and process the disappointment and anger will be necessary. Then, when you teach your children coping strategies, they remember to use their strengths, and they feel like they belong, they can settle down. Otherwise, if children try to change what can't be changed, they may give up on *all* change. You don't want that to happen.

Many Jews who survived concentration camps are profound examples of resiliency. Regina Schwarcova Pretter survived three and a half years at Auschwitz, beginning when she was just seventeen years old. She then lived a wonderful life full of joy. When asked about surviving and the quality of her life, she answered, "You fight for the things you can do something about, and you don't waste your energy on the things you can't control."[2] (This quote is worth memorizing!)

Attitudes Can Always Change

Resiliency is hardest when some things *can't* change. Lack of ability and skill is real, and sometimes all the practice and studying in the world won't improve children to the level they want. We must teach children that practice doesn't make things perfect. Perfect practice will help.

Illnesses are real. Dogs get hit by cars. Sports teams lose games. Dance outfits don't arrive in time for recitals. When families are resilient, these realities won't destroy children. There may be setbacks and a season of tears, whining, and anger. With healthy modeling and parenting, these seasons will be shorter.

Teaching children that they can always change their attitude toward things that can't be changed empowers them. And it will empower you! There's great hope and freedom in knowing something can be done. Knowing you can personally make changes results in optimism.[3] (How often have you read of optimism's value in these pages?)

Maddy's Power

When my young friend Maddy was able to see her dyslexia as a superpower, everything changed. Now she talks more about her creative abilities than her reading challenges. Resiliency allows her not to be defined by her challenges. She and her parents don't deny her dyslexia, but they also make sure she knows about her strengths. Their attitude is everything! Her parents and tutor have taught her she *has dyslexia* which is different from she *is dyslexic.*

Maddy and all children can learn coping strategies—"The best protection against unsafe, worrisome behaviors."[4] They are essential for hope to reign and attitudes to stay positive. Maddy's most critical coping strategies may be in dealing with the frustration. Yes, she needs strategies for overcoming spelling and reading difficulties. Her mom can provide many of these since she homeschools Maddy and her siblings. Being able to label her emotions, ask for specific help, distract herself when she's angry, avoid certain situations, and remember to use her strengths may be the most important coping strategies of all. If Maddy is occasionally embarrassed or angry, the emotional and intellectual pain doesn't last.

Not allowing children to be defined by labels or difficulties is a gift you teach. When you're present and you have an optimistic explanatory style, you'll help them know themselves. They'll believe your input because they know you're on their side. Maddy is known for her joy, perseverance, creativity, and passion for serving partly because this is what her parents tell others and talk with her about. She is not known for having dyslexia.

PLAN TO CHANGE THEIR SELF-TALK

Self-talk, your children's internal monologue, is something to try to observe when you're around them. Chances are good that if they've had many failure experiences and a pessimistic explanatory style, their self-talk is damaging. Talk with them about how powerfully destructive negative self-talk can be. Help them see that they may be stuck because of what they're believing and saying and not due to a true lack of skill, ability, or character.

But, if self-talk is internal, how can it be observed? You might hear some as they mutter under their breath. Those quiet thoughts originate in their minds and sometimes sneak out. Also, as you stay present and choose to become more in tune with their emotions, you'll be able to predict what they're saying to themselves.

Pay attention when your daughter follows you to her room so you can tell her if it's clean enough for her to invite a friend over. Does she mumble, *I bet she'll find a lot wrong again*? Her self-talk indicates that she thinks you're critical. This will affect her relationship with you. She may not be confident when she's around you.

When you notice your children hesitate to invest in themselves, ask them what they're thinking. Ask about their extreme thinking. For instance, how do they use the words "never" and "always"? *Boys will always be mean. My heart will always hurt. I'll always be anxious. I'll never be as good as everybody thinks I can be.*

The Power of "I Am . . ."

Ask how your children use the phrase "I am . . ." in their self-talk. For example, "I am a screwup" is substantially different from "I screwed up."[5] "I am never going to be loved" is different from "Seth doesn't love me anymore." And, remember what Maddy's parents have taught her. "I have dyslexia" is healthier than "I am dyslexic." Her parents passed their beliefs on to Maddy. This changes her internal dialogue, what she tells others, and how she behaves.

Children who constantly say "I'm a screwup" won't approach old tasks, new tasks, new situations, or people with confidence. Again, help them see how controlling this is. This belief could be a main reason these children are stuck.

The Power of "Yet"

Teaching children to add the transformative word "yet" to negative self-talk will be a gift.[6] *I am not loved* becomes *I am not loved yet.* And *I'm not good enough to make the team* becomes *I'm not good enough to make the team yet.* Do you see the hope and the power in this small word?

The word "yet" communicates growth. It reminds children that not everything is permanent. It is proof that resiliency is real. They can change their mindset and choose a recovery process from defeat and loss to victory and gain.

The Power of Asking for Specific Help

It's too hard! I can't do it! I'll never get better at this! I don't know how to do this! My friends will never think I'm cool! Do you hear complaints like these from any of your children? Some non-resilient children begin thinking these things before they even see the paper to complete or hear what chore you're assigning. If they're pessimistic and have many failure experiences, these beliefs can become deeply ingrained in their internal dialogue.

They verbalize these thoughts when they trust you. Or maybe it's just about getting your sympathy. This can become their way of getting you to do their work for them. After hearing "I can't do it" several times, many parents throw their hands up in frustration and just do it for their children. I get that. Remember my snowsuit example? If I had zipped zippers every time my students complained that they couldn't, I might still be zipping zippers. Not really, but you get my point.

Teach your children to ask for specific help when they're overwhelmed, confused, and scared of making mistakes.[7] Model this for your children. Acknowledging we don't know everything and asking for help are healthy dependence and resiliency attributes.

You can be present and repeat, "How can I help you?" Although you've read a lot about being aware of children's emotions, it's not best to engage their feelings if you know they can do something but they're whining to manipulate you. Rather, become the teacher and coach you want to be. "What don't you understand?" "What do you need?"

Encourage your children to change their self-talk from complaints to questions. When they believe something may be hard, they can ask themselves, "How can I get started?" "How is this similar to something I've done well?" "What strengths can I use?" "Which character qualities do I need to use?"

This type of self-talk empowers them to get started and keep working. Rather than focusing on mistakes and failure, it focuses their energy on progress.

PROVIDE HELPFUL FEEDBACK

Your compliments and corrections are among your best tools for influencing children's beliefs about themselves and, therefore, their behavior. Your evaluations also influence their self-talk because they can learn to model their internal thoughts after your compliments and corrections. For example, if they hear you talk about their joy often enough, maybe they'll start to see it too. Now you've empowered them to reject the lie they tell themselves—*I'm always depressed.*

Be More Positive than Negative

Being positive can secure children's hearts and make it more likely that they'll trust you with all that's going on in their world. Their resulting honesty and vulnerability will give you valuable information as you're building up their resiliency.

Zapping

Zapping is another negative communication pattern to avoid. You "zap" your children when you immediately follow a compliment with a criticism or put a critical word in a compliment.

For example, "Great job! You finally figured it out!" What word will cause your children to feel zapped? "Finally." This is a passive-aggressive way to let your children know you haven't been pleased with how they're doing.

Picture your son reacting to these comments: "Great job passing the ball to Kevin often during the first quarter. Why didn't you do it more in the second?" The compliment encourages your son and gives him hope that you're on his side. Your question can cause him to think, *I can never please my dad. He's never satisfied!* This communication pattern leads children to believe you're looking for perfection and can cause them to hide their mistakes and struggles.

Toxic Positivity

You might remember that optimism is a huge factor in children developing a healthy explanatory style for their struggles and trauma. "Optimism" comes from a Latin word meaning "best." Looking for the best and not the worst is wise and helpful. However, you must be optimistic without being toxic.

"Toxic positivity" is dangerous. It's "the belief that no matter how dire or difficult a situation is, people should maintain a positive mindset . . . Toxic positivity instead rejects difficult emotions in favor or a cheerful, often falsely positive, facade."[8]

If you've been on the receiving end of comments like, "You just have to be positive!" and "Stop being so negative!" you know how dismissed a person can feel. For your children to trust you, open up, admit to having experienced "little t" and "big T" trauma, and ask you for help, they need to know they'll be respected. Respect means they've been seen, heard, and taken seriously.

If you have recently shared toxic positivity comments like these, I'm sure you were well-intentioned. Do you see, though, how they prevent children from being open with you and believing you? If you want them to believe they can count on you, you will support them, and more, then speak carefully when they're struggling.

After a healthy discussion about what's going on, feeling your children's pain, and problem-solving together to change the future, you can say things like "You've got this!" Now your optimism won't feel dismissive. Of course, declare things like, "I'm listening," and "Your feelings are normal and understandable," and "Sometimes bad things happen."

Compliment Specifically

As I explain in *Start with the Heart*, the purpose of compliments is to get more of what you want.[9] If you say, "Good job!" your children may not know what they did well that they should do again. They can't read your mind.

General praise like this may encourage your children. But it may also discourage them because they don't know what to do to please you again. Specific praise is motivational and helps children try again after they're hurt and disappointed. Now they'll continue to learn and grow. If you don't affirm them at all or you're vague when you do, they may not make progress or be resilient.

Was your daughter more efficient and less frustrated because she was more organized? Tell her. Was your son's history paper better because he provided more support for his hypotheses? Tell him. Did your daughter have a better experience at youth group because she was kind and cooperative? Tell her. Did your son recover better from a challenging experience because he gamed less and spent time resting? Tell him.

Correct and Don't Criticize

In the same way, corrections must be specific. This makes them helpful so children can improve. It doesn't help to tell them, "Do it differently next time" or "Just get over it!"

To criticize is to point out an error. To correct is to put it right.[10]

If you want your children to be resilient, avoid criticizing them. You want them to improve so your intentions may be good. But children can't make changes if they only know what's wrong.

Resilient children are willing to try again, but they need to know how.

Criticisms are also damaging because they breed perfectionism. If your children think you can't be pleased, they'll hesitate to talk with you about their heartache and difficulties. Now you'll have fewer opportunities to influence them positively. Resiliency is less likely.

The Right Way to Correct

When you correct children by including instruction that helps them improve, you give them more than hope. You empower them because now they know what to do differently. You haven't just pointed out a problem; you helped to put it right.

Resilient children are willing to try again, but they need to know how. For example, instead of evaluating children with "Do it differently next time," which is a criticism because it only communicates that something was wrong, try statements like these: "Next time, ask for help when you get overwhelmed so you don't yell and stomp out of the room, which was embarrassing for you," or "Next time, remember you can stand up for yourself and say no rather than doing what everyone in the group was doing. You got in over your head and now it's hard for you to trust those friends again. We've talked about how I will support you in situations like that."

Recognize the Causes

Resilient children bounce back from trauma because they believe they can. Your feedback can teach them that! Children need to know how they contributed to their successes and what they did or didn't do that resulted in mistakes and failures.

In chapter 2, I made it clear that mistakes and failures can happen because of bad attitudes, unhealthy character, and lack of ability, experiences, or training. When you help children identify the causes, you direct their steps moving forward. This is partly because you can affect all three elements of their explanatory style—what they believe about who is responsible, how long effects of trauma will last, and how it will affect them.

CHANGE WORKS!

When you talk about children's successes, point out what they did that helped. It's not just that they're smart, but that they applied themselves. I like to say, "You were smart with your smarts!"[11] In the same way, when they disappoint themselves, help them see that they're not stupid. They just weren't being smart in the moment. If they believe they're stupid, they won't believe they can be resilient. These children tell me, "Studying (or using effort, asking for help, or practicing more) won't help me. Why should I bother? I'm just bad at this!" They need to know what they can do next time. They're not stuck!

For example, is your son suffering "little t" trauma because of a low grade that caused him to miss some basketball games due to his coaches' policies? Teammates are mad, coaches are disappointed, and he's depressed and angry with himself. You can ask your son what he thinks caused his grade to slip. Interact with him and tell him what you observed. Was he prideful and didn't think he needed to study? Did he game so much that he was tired and distracted when he did study? You want to increase his optimism by helping him make different decisions for upcoming math tests. He needs to know he's not stupid. Studying and changes in his character will help. He can grow. He's not stuck!

Depending on the type of trauma experienced, children might think, *I deserved what happened. I'm such a loser!* Perhaps your daughter was publicly embarrassed and isn't handling it well. Your feedback about the causes can help your daughter believe her unwise decisions at the lock-in were because of a lack of experience, she didn't discern what her friends were up to, and she was desperate to be popular. She needs you to help her learn from what happened. She can have positive future encounters. She's not stuck!

Your compliments and corrections are powerful tools. Use them well!

EMBRACE LIFE WITH CONFIDENCE

One of the easiest ways to get kids unstuck and moving toward the comeback they need is to simply talk about and model the benefits of challenges. Children who think everything should be easy and automatic, including recovery from hard things, will not be able to embrace life. They'll stay stuck.

Perhaps an example from the Chicago Cubs will help you and your children further understand that avoiding all challenges isn't wise. You might remember that the Cubs won the World Series in 2016 after a 108-year drought. I remember being so delighted for the team and fans. I followed the Cubs when I lived in Indiana and can still hear Harry Caray shout, "Holy cow!!"

President Theo Epstein gave credit to resiliency. Essentially, recruiting "failures" won them the championship. When talking about recruiting, he said, "We will always spend more than half the time talking about the person rather than the player . . . We would ask our scouts to provide three detailed examples of how these young players faced adversity on the field and responded to it, and three examples of how they faced adversity off the field. Because baseball is built on failure. The old expression is that even the best hitter fails seven out of ten times."[12]

Of course, inventors, athletes, and musicians are great examples of resilient people to talk with your children about. The successful ones didn't go from being unknown to famous and possibly wealthy overnight. Most people aren't aware of how long they struggled. They're known for their successes. They experimented, problem-solved, got help, and used effort, diligence, and perseverance to move from being stuck to unstuck, from failing to making progress to succeeding.

Your children will embrace life when they want to succeed badly enough to put in the work. They, too, can become unstuck!

Butterflies need their time in the chrysalis. The process of emerging is worth all the effort—they're beautiful.

In all toil there is profit, but mere talk tends only to poverty.
Proverbs 14:23

SPIRITUAL
Resiliency

My friend Amy completed her hospital chaplain residency at a big-city hospital in the Midwest during the first year of the COVID-19 pandemic. She then took a job as a hospital chaplain in the mountains out west.

In two years, Amy has seen more death than some hospital chaplains see in a career. Her social media updates and prayer requests have kept friends connected. I've been humbled and inspired by her faith. She is spiritually resilient.

Amy described a patient who was a strong believer who needed to be put on a ventilator as his health deteriorated. She wrote, "I prayed that as he walked through the dark valley he would strongly sense Jesus by his side and the Holy Spirit leading him beside still waters and making him lie down in green pastures."

Amy shared that when it was clear nothing was working, family members flew in and surrounded him. Amy shared, "So now we hold vigil knowing soon that absent from the body is present with the Lord. COVID didn't win. Jesus is stronger than death."

Yes, Jesus *is* stronger than death! Amy has years of experience with God and education to back up her current choices. She keeps choosing God even when her days and nights are long and difficult. We know adults with similar backgrounds who have given up on God. What makes the difference?

Consider this: Amy texted me on another difficult night about three weeks after posting the above. She wrote, "Pray that I accept the Lord's will. I am no different than Christians throughout history who've ministered to the sick and come down with illness and/or died. I knew that going in. God owes me nothing except to keep His covenant."

You can raise children who know and love Jesus this well. They don't have to doubt the goodness of God even during hard times. They can accept His will. They can have strong faith in the God of the Bible and be strong in Him and not themselves. What do they need to know and believe?

For children to have spiritual resilience, they need to know who the God of the Bible is. A broad, accurate understanding based on more than their favorite name of God and favorite verse will serve them well. They need to understand the value of spiritual disciplines and use them well to connect to God so that they love Him more deeply. They need an accurate theology of challenge and suffering. And, they need to be in relationships with genuine, authentic people they can be honest with—including you.[1]

DEAL WITH CHILDREN'S DOUBTS AND QUESTIONS

Because you've read that healthy relationships and resiliency go hand in hand, I hope you're already motivated to improve the quality of your family's belonging. Maybe you've already made some good changes. Congratulations!

Notice that I haven't written that you should be friends with your children. Healthy relationships that result in solid belonging mean it's more likely you'll be friends with your *adult* children. Prioritizing friendship when you're still in the throes of being their primary authority isn't wise.

Healthy relationships mean you put your children first when you should. You listen, teach, coach, correct, and compliment. You're available and work to be fully present. Although healthy relationships are essential for developing all types of resiliency, they may be most important when children have doubts and concerns relevant to their faith. If they know faith is important to you, it will feel precarious to admit their confusion.

Your children are bound to have some questions. You may have some even if you've had a relationship with God for a while.[2]

You've probably discovered that talking things over can facilitate understanding and bring assurance to places where doubts have reigned. For children to share what's bothering them so you can help them bounce back spiritually, your belonging needs to be solid. Always prioritize it.

Relationships with Others

Helping your teens find other adults to guide and lead them is wise. These friends and mentors can support your efforts and answer your children's questions when you're unavailable or they hesitate to be honest with you. Often these friends will have different experiences. And, if they're closer in age to your children, they'll sometimes better understand their temptations and confusion.

Choose not to be offended if your teens appear to value others' opinions more highly than yours. Yes, they still need to see you as an authority and they need to listen. But during adolescence, healthy teens usually look for ways to separate from their families to define themselves as individuals.[3]

As long as you know your children are leaning on like-minded people who are healthy role models, they'll benefit. You'll want to be alert to who they choose and orchestrate it so they get to know positive peers and adults.

If you allow your children to hang out with those who don't believe in God, who don't believe Jesus is the only way to heaven, or who believe differently about cultural issues, don't be surprised if they begin to question what they've been taught. As I point out in *Screens and Teens*, it's common for younger people to have re-lationship-based beliefs.[4] That's why many of us teach, "Show me your friends, and I'll show you your future."

> *Choose not to be offended if your teens appear to value others' opinions more highly than yours.*

My niece, Katie, my nephew, Andy, and his wife, Steph, all work with youth. They've seen the truth of this idea. As we talked, they groaned when they thought about youth who were persuaded by friends to reject teaching they had previously agreed with. Parents who contact me about way-ward children and prodigals almost always tell me about a peer or two who became very influential in their children's lives.

But it's not just friends in the traditional way. A reason to be fully present to your children and to plan intentional conversations is so you're aware of media and personalities your kids pay atten-tion to. Songs they memorize, shows they binge-watch, and stars they follow on social media all influence them and their beliefs.

Conversations

When children voice a doubt or indicate they're confused, remem-ber ideas from chapters 6 and 7. Wear your parent face and use "Keep talking" to get more information before reacting. Maybe ask for an example or comparison to help you understand. Is your daughter trying to understand someone who says she is against abortion, but for the death penalty? She thinks she's pro-life and your daughter isn't sure. Or maybe someone is pro-life but talks very negatively about special needs kids, which confuses your daughter.

First, acknowledge her confusion: "I'm sorry you're confused. I know you love it when everything makes sense." Thank her for trusting you and maybe ask her how you can help. Does she want to have a discussion? Look at Scripture together? Talk with the pastor? Invite you to share a relevant illustration from your life?

Listening is often more important than what you say. Being available counts for a lot. Remember, as I've written earlier, you don't have to have all the answers. In fact, you can't. Isaiah 40:28 informs us that God's "understanding is unsearchable." Children will respect you when you admit you don't understand something either and will work *with them* to get some answers. Because you're searching together, they'll learn how to discern truth from you.

Children will have doubts and questions before they trust Christ *as well as* after. Don't panic! Just like panicking is unwise when they don't know something or make mistakes in other realms, work to remain calm when their choices, behaviors, or questions about faith and God concern you.

If you become impatient with all their questions, panic, or get quickly angry, they may not share easily with you again. More importantly, they might assume God will react in the same way. If this has already been your response, I get it. These are your children and their eternal life is at stake! Talk with them. Apologize if you should. Ask them to trust you. Prove to them that you'll help them discern truth and walk with them while they search.

Habits

Like all parents, you have opinions about your children's choices. Just make sure they're fair. When children trust Christ as their Savior, some changes in their behaviors can be instant. Praise God! It often takes motivation, studying, and time with God and His people for Jesus Christ to also become their Lord.

For example, rarely will children automatically develop pure speech or quickly hate evil and pride.[5] The heart will need to be transformed to "act justly and to love mercy and to walk humbly with your God" (Mic. 6:8 NIV). Loving the "1 Corinthians 13 way" is foreign to many. Even after being discipled and knowing God, loving people God's way isn't easy.

When children trust Christ for their salvation or simply become more interested in God, your hope and expectations for righteous behavior increase. If you're not careful, this can cause you to be critical when your children's choices and behaviors don't change. This can confuse and anger them. If you know this has happened, is it possible you've judged them using unfair standards?

Even after being disciped and knowing God, loving people God's way isn't easy.

Can they behave the way you want them to, or do you just wish they could? Do they know God well enough to want to honor Him in their choices? Then, do they know how?

Apologize if it's warranted. Perhaps read the above paragraph to your children to help them understand your motives are right. Then talk about their first goals and how you can best help them mature in their understandings and behaviors.

As I've written often, changing behavior and beliefs is possible. Yet, we honor children when we remember that habits aren't easy to break. Maybe doubt has been a habit. Swearing. Drinking. Negativity. Despair. Temper tantrums. Hate. Judging. Self-centered choices. All habits.

A child learning to walk hasn't made a mistake when falling. In the same way, scribbling and baby talk aren't mistakes. These are proper phases children need to go through to learn coloring, handwriting, and talking. In the beginning, children learning to trust God and act on their faith may take two steps back for every forward step, but they haven't made mistakes either. They're simply progressing in their walk with Christ.

Your children's habits will break when you point out the specifics of what they're doing wrong and teach why the new way is better and more biblical. Talk more about who they are becoming than what they've been doing wrong. They're familiar with what they've been doing wrong; they need to learn more about what to do right. Everyone should know the end of Isaiah 1:16 and the beginning of Isaiah 1:17: "Stop doing wrong. Learn to do right" (NIV).

WHO CHILDREN THINK GOD IS

I came to faith in Christ because I had many questions about the Bible and God's ways.[6] God used Colossians 2:3 to move me from doubt to faith, insecure to secure, and unsaved to saved. This Word declares that "all the treasures of wisdom and knowledge" are hidden in Christ.

I'm glad I discovered God is so much more than this! If not, I would have only expected Him to provide answers to my questions and clarity for my confusion. My limiting beliefs about God would have diminished my hope and decreased my abundance. And, if I hadn't gotten answers to some questions, I might have given up on God. I might have thought He didn't love me, know me, or care about me.

To increase spiritual resiliency, teach your children how big and magnificent God is. Don't let them know only a favorite verse or two. Knowing Him more completely helps them know they can rely on Him and for what. Perhaps rather than giving up on Him when they're confused, overwhelmed, or disappointed, they'll think about a different attribute of God and move toward Him. Maybe they think He didn't appear to be faithful, but they can see that He was wise. They'll bounce back!

Teaching the names of God and His attributes are practical ways of introducing even young children to the whole of God. For example, God is the everlasting God, He provides for us, and He is our peace.[7] Jesus is the light of the world, indescribable gift, and authority.[8] God's attributes include that He is sovereign, long-suffering, and impartial.[9] Christ's attributes include that He is fair, dependable, and optimistic.[10] The Holy Spirit teaches, convicts, and intercedes for us.[11]

STRUGGLES CAN STRENGTHEN CHILDREN'S FAITH

In times of struggle and challenge, even mature believers may question whether God is good and loving. Children's questions are even more understandable because they don't understand God as deeply.

Adults' understandings are richer and our trust is deeper because we have known God longer and experienced more life with Him than children have. If you want your children to grow spiritually, don't hover over them or try to protect them from the world. Both will diminish their growth. They need experiences leaning on God to discover who He truly is.

Experiences help head knowledge gravitate to the heart. They'll help children gain confidence in what they've learned. God's attributes will become real. Doubts more quickly lift.

I think this is why when I ask my adult audiences if they have stronger character and faith because of the challenges, disappointments, and even heartache God allows them to experience, about 80 percent of the people quickly raise their hands to say yes. In tough times, we can learn God is who He says He is. We learn that needing Him is a good thing!

Teach your children that although God could make everything and everyone perfect, He intentionally doesn't. He understands the value of walking out of valleys and coming back from trauma.

If this is true, why do so many parents bubble-wrap their children and solve problems for them before they could have learned rich lessons? Are the parents weak and afraid? Do they not trust their children to learn from the experiences? Are they impatient and unwilling to do the sometimes-messy work of walking with their children? Do they not trust God?

Who Children Learn God Is

Spiritually non-resilient children are children who haven't experienced much of God. They haven't learned to depend on Him. They haven't been honest with Him. They may have head knowledge and Sunday school right answers. They may be able to pass a Bible quiz in a Christian school and answer Dad's questions right during a family devotion. But this can't be good enough!

Children will learn who God is when they don't run from their challenges. When you don't prevent messes or clean up their messes for them, they can discover how to rely on God. You must let your children live so they can see God act on their behalf. Just like we learn a lot about ourselves under pressure, we learn a lot about God when we're under pressure. So can our kids.

Do you remember the names and attributes I suggested teaching children? Teach them and then allow God to orchestrate their lives so they'll be proven true. Talk about these things and point them out to your children when they can't see them on their own. For example:

God is the everlasting God. Therefore, He won't give up on me. He won't get tired of my questions or needs.

God provides for me. He has given me time, talent, resources, people to help me, and even forced me to rest when I was sick.

God is my peace. I don't need to worry. He can take care of emotional turmoil, messy relationships, my physical concerns, and the intellectual confusion I'm dealing with.

Jesus is the light of the world. I don't have to live in the dark. Jesus can show me the way out of my dark place.

Jesus is an indescribable gift. I don't deserve Jesus' sacrifice and there's nothing I can ever do that would earn it. It's a gift! I can relax and stop performing.

Jesus is my authority. I need to humble myself, ask Him for help, read the Word, pray for wisdom, and follow His lead.

Continue this idea with the attributes listed earlier and other names and attributes from the resources listed in the endnotes or your resources. Do all you can to help children believe and see that God behaves the way He does because of who He is.

God is faithful. Therefore, He . . .

God is loving. Therefore, He . . .

God is impartial. Therefore, He . . .

Suffering Is a Part of God's Design

Children must learn that God is not a magic genie who does away with all evil and suffering. Verses like the following, men like Job, and heroes like Paul show us that tribulation, trials, and suffering exist and may touch us. That doesn't make God bad or unloving.

We rejoice in our sufferings, knowing that suffering produces endurance, and endurance produces character, and character produces hope, and hope does not put us to shame, because God's love has been poured into our hearts through the Holy Spirit who has been given to us. (Rom. 5:3–5)

Rejoice in hope, be patient in tribulation, be constant in prayer. (Rom. 12:12)

Count it all joy, my brothers, when you meet trials of various kinds, for you know that the testing of your faith produces steadfastness. And let steadfastness have its full effect, that you may be perfect and complete, lacking in nothing. (James 1:2–4)

You don't want children to assume that they will never experience disappointments and trauma. You can't afford for your children to believe that if they're experiencing hard times it's because God doesn't love them.

Some would say the exact opposite is true. Because God wants us to mature and become more like His Son, Jesus Christ, He may allow trauma to affect us. This is an important insight to share with children. Our suffering, pain, turmoil caused by significant disappointment, and more have meaning. There's purpose in it. God plans all for our good.

Teach your children what good can happen from your family's challenges and their individual pain. Character growth and lasting faith are huge gains! Let this inspire you: "Hurt is the pain we feel when our suffering seems meaningless. Austrian psychoanalyst Viktor Frankl, who survived a Nazi concentration camp, noticed that people bear up under pain as long as they see the meaning in it. If we understand why we're suffering, Frankl believed, it ceases to be suffering."[12] Powerful!

Also, teach your children that Jesus understands suffering, so they'll walk toward Him in times of need rather than run from Him. He can relate to their situation! In age-appropriate ways, make sure they know Jesus suffered on the cross for them. His death was brutal. Putting up with the pain in my foot and back when I serve Jesus is more manageable when I remember how much He suffered for me.

Teach children that Jesus cares about the brokenhearted: "The Lord is near to the brokenhearted and saves the crushed in spirit" (Ps. 34:18). "He heals the brokenhearted and binds up their wounds" (Ps. 147:3).

Teach children that God has overcome evil: "In the world you will have tribulation. But take heart; I have overcome the world" (John 16:33).

Teach children that Jesus raised children and adults from the dead. He healed many people. He fed the hungry and taught the lost. "He freed people tormented by demons. . . . Jesus didn't medicate suffering; he overcame it."[13]

Teach them God is working for our good (Rom. 8:28). God

has not forgotten about us (Heb. 6:10). God won't leave us (Deut. 31:8). God's love never fails (Rom. 8:39).

HOW RESILIENT CHILDREN RELATE TO GOD

I want to encourage you to think more about how children relate to God than you possibly have. Yes, as I've written, they need to know Him. They need to believe in Him. They need to understand as much about His ways and His will as possible. They need to keep growing in wisdom.

You and your teaching, conversations, and modeling help tremendously. So do hard times and their pain, suffering, disappointment, and confusion. God uses these to mature children and to want more of Him and from Him—when they're resilient. If they're not resilient and they've learned to run from hard things and difficult people, their spiritual growth will be affected.

How children's understandings affect their reactions to God and their relationship with Him are key. Through their choices, attitudes, and behaviors, they put their beliefs on display. Are they hungry for Him? Do they spontaneously bring God up in conversations? Have they relegated Him to Sundays only?

Relationship Should Rule

Christianity is different from other religions because it's about a relationship and not rules. It's about a person, not a system. This means how we relate to God, Jesus, and the Holy Spirit must be prioritized. Our walk is not about our knowledge; it's about our actions. Do you model this?

Your children benefit when you put your relationship with God, rather than your obedience, on display. From talking and listening, and observing your priorities and choices, they can learn that pursuing Christ matters most. Model your whole relationship—your dependence on Jesus as your provider, counselor, celebrator, healer, and more. Help your children pursue Jesus as their Savior, Lord, friend, righteousness, and more.

> *Your children benefit when you put your relationship with God, rather than your obedience, on display.*

Although our relationships with the God of the Bible and His Son are very different from other relationships, they are relationships. Relationships have an ebb and flow to them. There are peaks and valleys to friendships—times when we're in close contact with someone and times when we're not. Times when we can think of many things wrong with the person and times when we can't.

Although God would want us to be close to Him at all times, as He is close to us, there are times when the sin of self-sufficiency enters in. Or maybe we're not content with our circumstances and we blame God, so spending time with Him isn't appealing.

Busyness might take over and our habit of starting our days with Him and His Word dissipates.

Teach your children that these are regular happenings and they don't need to beat themselves up when this happens. They can bounce back! I know of many children and adults who relate to God through routines, and when the practices fail them, they quit. If they don't pray for three days in a row, they feel like such failures that they don't think they can pray again. They can pray on the fourth day!

Spiritual resiliency requires starting again and again and again. Children will be more likely to do this when a quality relationship with God is the goal. Therefore, model that Christianity is about our relationship with Jesus and not a religion for Jesus.

Your relationship with your children matters too. When children discover you won't reject them when they're honest with you about their issues, they can begin to believe God won't reject them. When they learn how to ask you for help rather than whine and complain, they might try to behave the same way toward God. When they learn how to receive and benefit from your correction, they will learn from God's more readily.

Rule-Based Religion

Maybe I'm convinced of the importance of our relationship with God and Christ because this isn't how my faith journey began. As

I wrote, I placed high value on God's wisdom. I wanted to understand what He wanted me to do. I wanted to be "good enough." I didn't fully embrace the beautiful truth that God's Son, Jesus Christ, sacrificed Himself for my salvation as a free gift I couldn't earn.

I was a rule follower. Even now, in my personal and professional life, I'm ordered, detailed, and prefer to know what's happening in advance. I don't like making mistakes. I've learned to have grace and mercy for myself, accept them from others, gratefully receive them from God, and willingly offer them to others. I'm grateful I can honestly say, "I'm glad Christianity is about a relationship even though it's messy at times."

Being rule-based is fatiguing. It invites legalism, judging, comparisons, and scorekeeping. In contrast, focusing on children's relationship with Jesus can be energizing and freeing. It allows you to talk about how their choices disappoint Jesus and break God's heart or bring Him glory. You can stay focused on the relationship at the center of their faith.

If your children fall, struggle, get angry, or feel lost, they know they can come back to Jesus. They've learned that relationships can be repaired and strengthened. Trying to bounce back to a rule doesn't work.

WANTING TO KNOW GOD BETTER

Because you want your children to prioritize their relationship with God so it grows, use disciplines like prayer, reading the Word, giving, serving, worship, confession, fellowship, and rest to disciple your children. This is what these disciplines are for! But make them about Jesus and not rules. Don't present them as burdens required of us. Make these about your children's relationship with Jesus. Help them see that they'll *want* to do these things because they want to have a great relationship with their Father, Savior, and Lord. These disciplines are not tasks they check off a list when they've done them. Of course, you'll have to adopt the same approach. Watch out! All of you might see an increase in your faith and in your love for God.

As I wrote in *Five to Thrive*, my pastor, Dr. Stephen Lowrie, "suggests we don't think of the things Christians do as Christian disciplines, but as relational activities instead. Rather than thinking of needing to be disciplined to do them, he wants us motivated by our relationship with God and our desire to strengthen it."[14]

This change in wording has been huge for me! I believe if my faith journey had started with "relational activities because I want to get to know God better" instead of "things I have to do to please God," I'd have greater wisdom from God and love for God today.

With spiritual disciplines, don't ask your children if they've "done them" with the threat of punishment in your voice if they haven't. This makes conversations about spiritual growth difficult. Instead, ask, "How did you benefit from spending time with Jesus today? What activity helped you relate well?" "Which relational activity do you want to use tomorrow? What are you looking forward to?" "The last time you worshiped God, how did you know that's what you were doing?" Have them ask you similar questions.

When explaining the activities to your children, emphasize the "why to" more than the "how to." They can watch you and others to figure out how to do them. And, of course, you can teach them what's important. But, understanding the purpose of prayer, worship, and the other practices will help the most.

Be careful and biblical! I believe a significant reason people of all ages give up on God and the church is a misunderstanding about who God is and how our faith journey can look. If your children expect something more than is appropriate from their relationship with God, giving up is easy. (Read that again.)

Prayer

Let me use prayer as an example of what I mean. If children believe prayer is simply asking for things they want or need, they'll treat God like an ATM or Amazon Prime. They have one expectation— to get exactly what they ordered immediately.

If God doesn't do that, they may assume God isn't real, isn't good, or doesn't love them. The keys are knowing God and His character, including that His love doesn't mean we get what we think we need when we think we need it, and what the activity of prayer is and how it works.

What do you think prayer is? When do your children hear and see you pray? Only at meals and never vulnerably? Only for others and never for your family? Only for your family and never for others? Only asking and never thanking? What you believe about prayer shows up in your actions and will influence your children. And, of course, what you believe about God shows up here, too.

I'm a fan of the "PART" prayer method advocated by Becky Tirabassi.[15] Our prayer life should consist of times of praising God for who He is, admitting our sins, requesting God meet needs, and thanking Him for what He has done. For me, separating praising God from thanking God has been huge.

Is this making sense? Whole books have been written about prayer and other relational activities. My purpose here is not to define and explain them all, but to show you that they can cause your children to have a vibrant, growing, meaningful relationship with the God of the Bible or not. A lack of understanding can cause children to give up on God, themselves, and the church. They're very related to resiliency.

Other Relational Activities

Have you told and taught your children why you read the Bible? Why do you study it and maybe memorize some verses? Do you "have to" or "want to"? Is it part of a religious routine or a relationship? Spending time with God helps you get to know Him just like spending time with family and friends helps you get to know them.

I know people who don't start reading through the Bible in January because they tell me they know they won't be consistent. Their fear of failure and unawareness that they can be resilient and pick up the Bible and start again has them trapped. They're fearful and picture God judging them. I've had to guard myself against these thoughts.

If these are your children, how can you help them? Model that you just start again after taking a break. Let them know how you process your disappointments. Talk more about the future blessings than disappointments about the past. Talk about reading verses rather than reading "the Bible." Some children have told me they don't start because they can't imagine reading the whole book. Read with them. Let them hear you pray for them and their desire to relate well to God. Teach them they can be spiritually resilient.

For all the activities, be realistic and honest. If you make it sound like every time you read Scripture you get a strong word from God, a revelation, or a solution to a problem, your children might wonder what's wrong with them when they don't. Let's be honest and let them know that some times in the Word are better than others. Remember, relationships have peaks and valleys. On the day I'm writing this, I had a fabulous lunch with a former member of the Celebrate Kids board of directors. We hadn't seen each other in a few years. Our time was refreshing for both of us. We were encouraged and we're looking forward to seeing each other again in six months. But not every conversation goes that way.

Let your children know when you have a meaningful worship experience and when you don't. Did your preparation influence the outcome? Were the songs the congregation sang just not your favorites? How does that matter? Was the pastor's message not personally as relevant as others? How did you stay engaged? Why will you go back to church even after a less-than-great experience?

You get the idea. We use the relational activities because they're biblical and they keep us connected to the God of the Bible. When that's what your children want, they'll pursue Christ even if it means walking through valleys, climbing over barriers, and battling things that distract them.

EMBRACE LIFE WITH CONFIDENCE

Many years ago, as I was reading through the Bible, I came to chapter 23 in the Old Testament book of Joshua. He was old and gathered leaders to himself to instruct them in how to carry on his work. I realized how comfortable I was with verses 6–10. They were a "do this" and "don't do this" format coupled with reminders of what God would do on their behalf. I thought, "I could check these off the list. One-and-done. Great!"

Then I read verse 11. I stopped as I registered the truth. Now it was as if the verse was in bold, neon, blinking lights. What was the verse? "Be very careful, therefore, to love the LORD your God."

I believe God wanted me to see this truth—to get things done, love God! Love isn't just the motivation. It's the equipping. It's the power. "Be very careful . . ." Joshua could have continued with "do the job well." "Get the work done." But, he didn't. He instructed the men to "love the LORD your God."

I believe God wanted me to see this truth—to get things done, love God!

Talk with your children about the love they have for God. How would they describe it? Weak? Strong? Devoted? Ambivalent? Forced and fake? Growing?

Ask your children if they want to love God more. Why or why not? How do they know how much or how well they love God? If they want to love Him more, how do they think they could do that?

> The LORD is my shepherd, I shall not want.
> He makes me lie down in green pastures.
> He leads me beside still waters.
> He restores my soul.
> He leads me in paths of righteousness
> for his name's sake.
> Even though I walk through the valley of the shadow of death,
> I will fear no evil,
> for you are with me;

your rod and staff,
they comfort me.
You prepare a table before me
in the presence of my enemies;
you anoint my head with oil;
my cup overflows.
Surely goodness and mercy shall follow me
all the days of my life,
and I shall dwell in the house of the LORD
forever.
Psalm 23

ONE LAST THOUGHT

Teaching and equipping children to be resilient moves them from the damaging, dangerous, and defeating "I won't" to the empowering, freeing, and affirming "I am." May God richly bless you as you parent children with this goal!

I won't.

I can't.

I don't know how.

I wish I could.

I think I might.

I might.

I think I can.

I can.

I think I will.

I will.

I did.

I am.

APPENDIX
Beliefs Resilient Children Have About THEMSELVES and Their PARENTS

RESILIENT CHILDREN BELIEVE THESE THINGS ABOUT THEMSELVES

I have value.

I'm worth investing in.

Hard work will pay off.

I can do this.

Effort won't kill me.

Everything that happens to me isn't my fault.

What I'm working on may not always be this hard.

My trauma experiences won't define or control me.

Learning is valuable.

My future can be bright.

Perfection isn't the goal. Progress is.

Positive affirmations don't make me prideful.

My strengths will help me when things are hard.

I won't let my weaknesses win. I can still fulfill my purpose.

"I messed up" is healthier than "I'm a mess-up."

The glass is half-full, not half-empty. I'm not in denial. I know it isn't full.

I can be joyful even when something is hard.

I know when to change course, change goals, or stop working on something.

Needing to stop doesn't always mean I failed or I'm a failure.

I can learn from my mistakes.

Hard things are opportunities for growth.

I can always change my attitude.

My character is important.

Asking for help doesn't mean I'm stupid. It means I care.

I may not be able to do everything I want to do.

What would you add?

RESILIENT CHILDREN BELIEVE THESE THINGS ABOUT THEIR PARENTS

My parents will help and encourage me.

My parents will love me no matter what.

My parents will forgive me and not constantly remind me of my past sin.

My parents won't reject me when I mess up.

My parents make mistakes, too.

My parents will ask me to forgive them when they sin against me.

My parents understand how I feel.

My parents handle disappointment, defeat, and challenge well.

My parents work hard to bounce back from disappointments.

My parents are consistent, stable, and dependable.

My parents let me struggle sometimes because they know it's good for me.

My parents will not rescue me from all consequences for the poor decisions I make.

My parents understand most learning is a process and not an easy one-and-done experience.

My parents are honest and trustworthy.

My parents' hope is rooted in God and not in my performances.

My parents turn to God during tough times and expect Him to meet their needs.

What would you add?

ACKNOWLEDGMENTS

My mom and dad were excellent parents and I'll always be grateful. They raised my brother, Dave, and me to know who we are and to develop our personalities and skills. They paid attention to our daily efforts and our performances. They helped us dream about our futures, worked with us when we needed help, commiserated with us when we faced disappointments, and celebrated our achievements.

When our mom was near death she told Dave and me how important it was to her that we stay united and committed to each other. Of course, we responded that we would and that our family would continue being a family although she would soon join our dad in heaven and no longer be with us. Dave made it clear that I could always depend on him. He has kept his word. I'm grateful.

Dave and my precious sister-in-law, Debbie, are my fabulous family. They help me be resilient—like my parents, they support my dreams, help me, commiserate with me without allowing me to stay in the valley, and celebrate what God enables me to accomplish. They are the best! Their children and their spouses also have my back. Their love strengthens me!

As always, I've been well supported by the Celebrate Kids Board of Directors. They have consistently demonstrated love, truth, grace, and mercy through the years. If they wouldn't, taking risks would be difficult. I'm grateful for their trust.

My staff is fantastic! Celebrate Kids and our conferences running under our Ignite the Family banner are healthy because of their talent, time, and investment. I'm very grateful to John Hannigan, Melissa Hannigan, Debbie Thompson, Tami Bister, and Evan Hampton. I especially appreciate John's creativity, courage, networking, ability to multitask without getting stressed, and confidence in God! He has been an answer to many prayers.

I'm also very grateful to people who pray for me and the ministry and to those who financially contribute to our cause. They are largely responsible for the good God allows us to achieve. I'm also surrounded by excellent thinkers who make me a better person. And Dr. Hanby, Dr. Gideon, and Linda Miller—my doctor, chiropractor, and fitness trainer—keep me healthy.

I'm also thankful for speakers and writers who partner with

us—too numerous to mention—who help us influence thousands of parents. My agents at Premiere Speakers Bureau are significant members of our team. I'm able to write books because all these people do what they do so well.

I have intentionally partnered with Moody Publishers to publish my thoughts and to support our conferences. The people are excellent and they get who I am and what all of us at Celebrate Kids want to accomplish. Their choice to trust me and my team increases my influence and I'm grateful.

Of course, God is my hope and my purpose! I do what I do because of Him, I am who I am because of Him, and I owe Him everything.

NOTES

Foreword

1. John A. Shedd, *Salt from My Attic* (Portland, ME: Mosher Press, 1928); quoted in *The Yale Book of Quotations*, ed. Fred R. Shapiro (New Haven, CT: Yale University Press, 2006), 705.

Chapter 1—What Is Resiliency and Why Does It Matter?

1. Kenneth Ginsburg and Martha Jablow, *Building Resilience in Children and Teens: Giving Kids Roots and Wings*, 4th ed. (Itasca, IL: American Academy of Pediatrics, 2020), 26.
2. Gail Gazzelle, *Everyday Resilience: A Practical Guide to Build Inner Strength and Weathering Life's Challenges* (Emeryville, CA: Rockridge Press, 2020), xii, 6. See also *The Road to Resilience* (brochure, Washington, DC: American Psychological Association and Bethesda, MD: Discovery Communications, Inc.).
3. Michael Neenan, *Developing Resilience: A Cognitive-Behavioural Approach*, 2nd ed. (New York: Routledge, 2018), 5–6.
4. Kathy Koch, *Five to Thrive: How to Determine If Your Core Needs Are Being Met (and What to Do When They're Not)* (Chicago: Moody Publishers, 2020), 111. See also Kathy Koch, *Start with the Heart: How to Motivate Your Kids to Be Compassionate, Responsible, and Brave (Even When You're Not Around)* (Chicago: Moody Publishers, 2019), 24.
5. Koch, *Five to Thrive*, see especially chapter 4.
6. Gazzelle, *Everyday Resilience*. See also Ginsburg and Jablow, *Building Resilience in Children and Teens*, especially chapter 5, and Marcus Warner and Stefanie Hinman, *Building Bounce: How to Grow Emotional Resilience* (Carmel, IN: Deeper Walk

International, 2018), especially chapter 1.

7. 1 Thessalonians 5:17.

8. Elena Aguilar, "What Does a Resilient Educator Do? Three Actions Separate Those Who Thrive from Those Who Merely Survive," *Educational Leadership* 79, no. 2 (October 2021): 2, and Sheryl Sandberg and Adam Grant, *Option B: Facing Adversity, Building Resilience, and Finding Joy* (New York: Alfred A. Knopf, 2017), 29.

9. Aguilar, "What Does a Resilient Educator Do?," 76–77. See also *The Road to Resilience*, Gazzelle, *Everyday Resilience*, and Daniel Siegel and Tina Bryson, *The Yes Brain: How to Cultivate Courage, Curiosity, and Resilience in Your Child* (New York: Bantam Books, 2019), 80.

10. Jessica Lahey, *The Gift of Failure: How the Best Parents Learn to Let Go So Their Children Can Succeed* (New York: Harper, 2015), 54.

11. Koch, *Start with the Heart*, 23–26.

12. Ginsburg and Jablow, *Building Resilience in Children and Teens*, 43.

Chapter 2—What Do Resilient Children Believe and Why Does It Matter?

1. Lesley Brown, ed., *The New Shorter Oxford English Dictionary on Historical Principles*, vol. 1 (New York: Oxford University Press, 1993), 1794.

2. Ibid., 907.

3. Stuart Flexner in association with the editors of the *Reader's Digest, Family Word Finder: A New Thesaurus of Synonyms and Antonyms in Dictionary Form* (Pleasantville, NY: Readers' Digest Association, 1975), 289.

4. This was the most common conclusion from an informal poll on Dr. Kathy's personal Facebook page.

5. Brown, *The New Shorter Oxford English Dictionary*, vol. 2, 3128.

6. Jill Savage and Kathy Koch, *No More Perfect Kids: Love Your Kids for Who They Are* (Chicago: Moody Publishers, 2013), 14, 22–23, 26–33.

7. Ibid., 23–26.

8. Ginsburg and Jablow, *Building Resilience in Children and Teens*, 94–95.

9. Jessica Lahey, *The Gift of Failure: How the Best Parents Learn to Let Go So Their Children Can Succeed* (New York: Harper, 2015), xi.

10. Ibid.

11. Ibid., xv.

12. Elyssa Barbash, "Different Types of Trauma: Small 't' versus Large 'T'," March 13, 2017, https://www.psychologytoday.com/us/blog/trauma-and-hope/201703/different-types-trauma-small-t-versus-large-t. See also Samantha Lande, "We Need to Talk About Little 't' Trauma—Here's What It Looks Like and How to Process It," June 25, 2021, https://www.realsimple.com/health/mind-mood/emotional-health/what-is-little-t-trauma.

13. Ibid.

Chapter 3—What Do Children Think About What Happened and Why Does It Matter?

1. Kenneth Ginsburg and Martha Jablow, *Building Resilience in Children and Teens: Giving Kids Roots and Wings*, 4th ed. (Itasca, IL: American Academy of Pediatrics, 2020), 109–13. See also Sheryl Sandberg and Adam Grant, *Option B: Facing Adversity, Building Resilience, and Finding Joy* (New York: Alfred A. Knopf, 2017), 16, and Martin Seligman et al., *The Optimistic Child: Proven Steps to Safeguard Children against Depression and Build Lifelong Resilience* (Boston: Houghton Mifflin Company, 1995), 162–93.

2. Seligman et al., *The Optimistic Child*, 52–63.

3. Kathy Koch, *Five to Thrive: How to Determine If Your Core Needs Are Being Met (and What to Do When They're Not)* (Chicago: Moody Publishers, 2020), see chapter 8. (The Celebrate Kids change process is based on Ephesians 4:22–24.)

4. Gail Gazzelle, *Everyday Resilience: A Practical Guide to Build Inner Strength and Weathering Life's Challenges* (Emeryville, CA: Rockridge Press, 2020), 52. See also Ginsburg and Jablow, *Building Resilience in Children and Teens*, 110.

5. See chapter 9 where I'll address spiritual resiliency.

6. Vince Lombardi, "Famous Quotes by Vince Lombardi," http://www.vincelombardi.com/quotes.html.

Chapter 4—How Struggling Helps Us

1. Marcus Warner and Stefanie Hinman, *Building Bounce: How to Grow Emotional Resilience* (Carmel, IN: Deeper Walk International, 2018), 10.

2. Kathy Koch, *Five to Thrive: How to Determine If Your Core Needs Are Being Met (and What to Do When They're Not)* (Chicago: Moody Publishers, 2020), 71–72, 74–79. See also Kathy Koch, *Start with the Heart: How to Motivate Your Kids to Be Compassionate, Responsible, and Brave (Even When You're Not Around)* (Chicago: Moody Publishers, 2019), 13–29, 40.

3. Jessica Lahey, *The Gift of Failure: How the Best Parents Learn to Let Go So Their Children Can Succeed* (New York: Harper, 2015), 53.

4. Kenneth Ginsburg and Martha Jablow, *Building Resilience in Children and Teens: Giving Kids Roots and Wings*, 4th ed. (Itasca, IL: American Academy of Pediatrics, 2020), 39.

5. Ibid.

6. Daniel Siegel and Tina Bryson, *The Yes Brain: How to Cultivate Courage, Curiosity, and Resilience in Your Child* (New York: Bantam Books, 2019), 52–53.

7. Ibid.

8. Koch, *Start with the Heart*, see chapter 2.

9. Ibid., 195–201.

10. Siegel and Bryson, *The Yes Brain*, 52–53.

11. Lahey, *The Gift of Failure*, xii.

12. Jessica Lahey, "Why Parents Need to Let Their Children Fail," January 29, 2013, https://

www.theatlantic.com/national/archive/2013/01/why-parents-need-to-let-their-children-fail/272603/.

13. For example, Helen Keller, J.K. Rowling, Albert Einstein, Elvis Presley, Thomas Edison, the Beatles, Walt Disney, Dr. Seuss, Abraham Lincoln, Henry Ford, and Michael Jordan.

14. Summit.org. Summit Ministries' mission is to equip and support rising generations to embrace God's truth and champion a biblical worldview.

Chapter 5—Yes, But . . .

1. Dave Roever with Kathy Koch, *Scarred* (Fort Worth, TX: Roever Communications, 1995).

2. Father God, direct the readers to know what's best for them to do. If they need to process difficulties from their past, please show them what is holding them back and how to move forward. Show them who can help them. Give them the courage and humility they need. Amen.

3. Mimi Swartz, "The Cheerleader Murder Plot," *Texas Monthly*, May 1991, https://www.texasmonthly.com/arts-entertainment/the-cheerleader-murder-plot/.

Chapter 6—How to Have Conversations That Build Resiliency

1. Kathy Koch, *Five to Thrive: How to Determine If Your Core Needs Are Being Met (and What to Do When They're Not)* (Chicago: Moody Publishers, 2020).

2. "Building Your Resilience," American Psychological Association, February 1, 2020, https://www.apa.org/topics/resilience.

3. Arlene Pellicane, *Parents Rising: 8 Strategies for Raising Kids Who Love God, Respect Authority, and Value What's Right* (Chicago: Moody Publishers, 2018), see strategy 6.

4. Kathy Koch, *Screens and Teens: Connecting with Our Kids in a Wireless World* (Chicago: Moody Publishers, 2015), 62–63.

Chapter 7—What to Say: Conversations That Build Resiliency

1. You can download this for free from the book's website so you can refer to it often.

2. Kathy Koch, *Start with the Heart: How to Motivate Your Kids to Be Compassionate, Responsible, and Brave (Even When You're Not Around)* (Chicago: Moody Publishers, 2019), 181–82.

3. Proverbs 1:5; 5:12–14; 7:24–25; 12:15; 13:1–3, 15, 31–32; 19:20.

4. Sheryl Sandberg and Adam Grant, *Option B: Facing Adversity, Building Resilience, and Finding Joy* (New York: Alfred A. Knopf, 2017), 43.

5. Romans 12:15.

6. Sandberg and Grant, *Option B*, 63.

7. Kenneth Ginsburg and Martha Jablow, *Building Resilience in Children and Teens: Giving Kids Roots and Wings*, 4th ed. (Itasca, IL: American Academy of Pediatrics, 2020), 140–47.

8. Jill Savage and Kathy Koch, *No More Perfect Kids: Love Your Kids for Who They Are* (Chicago: Moody Publishers, 2013), 99–100, 219–21.

9. Elizabeth Scott, "Cognitive Distortions and Stress," Verywell Mind, November 24, 2020, https://www.verywellmind.com/cognitive-distortions-and-stress-3144921.

10. Michael Neenan, *Developing Resilience: A Cognitive-Behavioural Approach*, 2nd ed. (New York: Routledge, 2018), 78.

11. Koch, *Start with the Heart*, 186–87.

12. Jessica Lahey, *The Gift of Failure: How the Best Parents Learn to Let Go So Their Children Can Succeed* (New York: Harper, 2015), 56.

13. Proverbs 4:10–11; 8:8–9; 10:18–20; 12:17–19; 16:23–24; 22:11–13.

14. Ginsburg and Jablow, *Building Resilience in Children and Teens*, 192.

15. I'm grateful for the inspiration for this section from Ginsburg and Jablow, *Building Resilience in Children and Teens*, 192.

16. Lori Wildenberg, *Messy Hope: Help Your Child Overcome Anxiety, Depression, or Suicidal Ideation* (Birmingham, AL: New Hope Publishers, 2021), 48–60.

17. Esther is an amazing young woman, and her story is one of remarkable courage and God's sovereignty. If anyone thinks the Bible is boring, I recommend reading this Old Testament book. It's far from boring!

18. This is a popular Japanese proverb. See "Fall Down Seven Times, Stand Up Eight," Mental Toughness Partners, September 2, 2018, https://www.mentaltoughness.partners/fall-down-seven-times-get-up-eight/.

Chapter 8—Get Unstuck: Moving from Setback to Comeback

1. Kenneth Ginsburg and Martha Jablow, *Building Resilience in Children and Teens: Giving Kids Roots and Wings*, 4th ed. (Itasca, IL: American Academy of Pediatrics, 2020), 345.

2. Ibid.

3. Ibid., 47.

4. Ibid., 46.

5. Brené Brown, *Rising Strong: How the Ability to Reset Transforms the Way We Live, Love, Parent, and Lead* (New York: Random House, 2017), 213.

6. Ginsburg and Jablow, *Building Resilience in Children and Teens*, 54. See also Carol Dweck, *Mindset: The New Psychology of Success* (New York: Ballantine Books, 2007).

7. Kathy Koch, *Start with the Heart: How to Motivate Your Kids to Be Compassionate, Responsible, and Brave (Even When You're Not Around)* (Chicago: Moody Publishers, 2019), 195–201.

8. Kendra Cherry, "What Is Toxic Positivity?," Verywell Mind, February 1, 2021, https://www.verywellmind.com/what-is-toxic-positivity-5093958.

9. Koch, *Start with the Heart*, 207–208, 212–13, and 265–67.

10. Ibid., 209–11, 213–16, 269–71.

11. Kathy Koch, *8 Great Smarts: Discover and Nurture Your Child's Intelligences* (Chicago: Moody Publishers, 2016).

12. Sheryl Sandberg and Adam Grant, *Option B: Facing Adversity, Building Resilience, and Finding Joy* (New York: Alfred A. Knopf, 2017), 150–51.

Chapter 9—Spiritual Resiliency

1. Check out Barna.org for excellent resources and research about what young people believe about God and the church. These books will also help you understand how the confusing culture affects teens and adults: Jeff Myers, *The Secret Battle of Ideas About God: Overcoming the Outbreak of Five Fatal Worldviews* (Colorado Springs: David C. Cook, 2017) and John Stonestreet and Brett Kunkle, *A Practical Guide to Culture: Helping the Next Generation Navigate Today's World* (Colorado Springs: David C. Cook, 2017).

2. I hope you know God personally and have trusted Christ for your salvation. He makes all the difference! Please read Romans 3:23, Romans 6:23, Romans 5:8, Romans 10:9, and Ephesians 2:8–9, and talk with people you know about your doubts and confusions.

3. Daniel P. Huerta, *Seven Traits of Effective Parenting* (Colorado Springs: David C. Cook, 2019).

4. Kathy Koch, *Screens and Teens: Connecting with Our Kids in a Wireless World* (Chicago: Moody Publishers, 2015), 38–42.

5. Proverbs 8:13.

6. Know your children so you know how to present the God of the Bible in ways that will interest them. In my book *8 Great Smarts*, I explain that my logic smart strengths prioritized my desire for wisdom. In each chapter about the smarts, I explain how you can talk about God so children will listen and learn.

7. Genesis 21:33, Genesis 22:14, Judges 6:24. Also, look for a more complete list of names of God on the book's website.

8. John 8:12, 2 Corinthians 9:15, Matthew 28:18. Also, look for a more complete list of names of Christ on the book's website.

9. Isaiah 46:10, Nahum 1:3, and Deuteronomy 10:17. Also, look for a more complete list of God's attributes on the book's website.

10. Matthew 7:12, 1 Corinthians 4:2, Romans 8:25. Also, look for a more complete list of Christ's attributes on the book's website.

11. John 14:26, John 16:7–8, Romans 8:26–27. Also, look for a more complete list of the Holy Spirit's roles on the book's website.

12. Jeff Myers, *The Secret Battle of Ideas About God*, 76.

13. Ibid., 92.

14. Kathy Koch, *Five to Thrive: How to Determine If Your Core Needs Are Being Met (and What to Do When They're Not)* (Chicago: Moody Publishers, 2020), 184.

15. Becky Tirabassi, *Let Prayer Change Your Life* (Newport Beach, CA: Change Your Life, Inc., 2015).

ABOUT KATHY KOCH, PHD, and CELEBRATE KIDS, INC.

Dr. Kathy Koch (pronounced "cook") is the Founder of Celebrate Kids, Inc., based in Fort Worth, TX. She has influenced thousands of parents, teachers, and children in 30 countries through keynote messages, seminars, chapels, conferences, and other events. She is proud to be represented by the Premiere Speakers Bureau of Nashville, TN. She is a featured speaker for Teach Them Diligently and a regular presenter for Care Net, Summit Ministries, the Colson Center, and other organizations. She speaks regularly at schools, churches, and pregnancy resource centers.

Dr. Kathy is also a popular guest on Focus on the Family radio and other radio talk shows and podcasts. Kirk Cameron chose her as an educational expert in his documentary, *Kirk Cameron Presents: The Homeschool Awakening*, and a technology expert in his 2018 movie, *Connect: Real Help for Parenting Kids in a Social Media World.* This is her sixth book for Moody Publishers. The others are *Five to Thrive, Screens and Teens, 8 Great Smarts, Start with the Heart*, and *No More Perfect Kids* (with Jill Savage).

Celebrate Kids partners with parents to strengthen family relationships, develop children's unique gifts and talents, and equip them to live on purpose with intentionality. They conduct Ignite the Family women's conferences and Redirected Parenting Conferences. Dr. Kathy and the Celebrate Kids team present a variety of topics at conventions, churches, schools, and for organizations. They also meet needs through an extensive product line, social media, podcasts, and a weekly email newsletter.

Dr. Kathy earned a PhD in reading and educational psychology from Purdue University. She was a tenured associate professor of education at the University of Wisconsin–Green Bay, a teacher of second graders, a middle school coach, and a school board member before becoming a full-time conference and keynote speaker in 1991. She has loved Jesus for years and her faith and desire to serve and glorify God is the foundation of her ministry.

Website: www.CelebrateKids.com
Facebook: www.facebook.com/celebratekidsinc
Instagram: www.instagram.com/celebratekidsinc
Podcast: *Celebrate Kids with Dr. Kathy*

DO YOU NEED A BREAKTHROUGH?

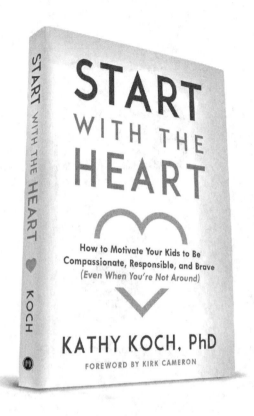

START WITH THE HEART

How to Motivate Your Kids to Be Compassionate, Responsible, and Brave *(Even When You're Not Around)*

KATHY KOCH, PhD

FOREWORD BY KIRK CAMERON

MOODY Publishers

From the Word to Life

Dr. Kathy Koch will teach you proven strategies that move your child from, "I can't, I won't," to "I can, I will, and I did." We can do better than behavior modification. We can change our children's hearts and teach them to be motivated toward godly and good goals.

978-0-8024-1885-2 | also available as an eBook

YOUR CHILD IS SMART, BUT DOES HE OR SHE *BELIEVE* IT?

YOUR UNMET NEEDS ARE AN INVITATION FROM GOD

MOODY Publishers

From the Word to Life

How do we find authentic hope and wholeness based on God's truth and reality? Dr. Kathy Koch draws on decades of seminars and workshops geared to the educational community to show us how intelligence and worth take different forms in each of us while having their ultimate roots in Jesus.

978-0-8024-1961-3 | also available as eBook and audiobook

IF YOU FEEL LIKE YOU'RE LOSING YOUR TEEN TO TECHNOLOGY, YOU'RE NOT ALONE.

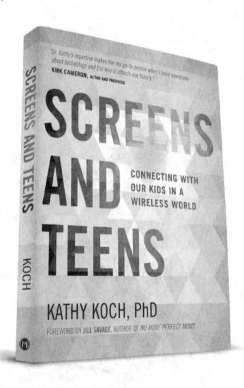